THE R100 INVESTOR

How Young South Africans Build Wealth One Month At A Time

Senzo J Hlangu

The characters and events portrayed in this book are fictitious. Any similarity to real persons, living or dead, is coincidental and not intended by the author.

ISBN-13: 9781234567890
ISBN-10: 1477123456

Cover design by: Art Painter
Library of Congress Control Number: 2018675309
Printed in the United States of America

To my family for the support and patience

CONTENTS

FOREWORD

When you walk into a Shoprite or Pick n Pay, what do they offer you to build a future? A Lotto ticket. Not an investment plan. A gamble.

When you open your banking app—Capitec or GoTyme or any banking app —what wealth-building tool stares back at you? The Lotto.

When you scroll through your phone, what does Vodacom conveniently offer you? Betway bucks.

The message is clear: if you want to get rich, your best bet—quite literally—is to gamble.

Not invest. Not grow. Gamble.

It's almost laughable if it weren't so tragic.

Banking has been democratised. Funeral policies are sold everywhere. Loans and credit products are offered aggressively by a multitude of providers. The tools for basic financial transactions and risk management are in the hands of the masses.

Yet, where are the investment products?

Betway sponsors our premier soccer league. Vodacom gives its customers direct access to gambling through its app. The same app we use to buy data. They're not even pretending anymore. You should not have wealth.

The Lotto sits in every banking app. It's like the banks are saying, "You want to be rich? Here, have a Lotto ticket. Good luck."

Because clearly, the path to wealth is picking six numbers and praying to your ancestors.

"You want to build wealth? Here, bet on the Chiefs game instead."

But what about building *actual* wealth?

Are South Africans simply not meant to build wealth? Are we only meant to consume, to gamble, and to rely on a compulsory employer retirement fund that we don't understand and rarely think about?

"Don't worry about building your own wealth. Just work for 40 years and hope your pension fund board of trustees and fund managers know what they're doing. And while you wait, why not place a bet?"

This is a massive opportunity for young South Africans, families and the country as a whole.

It is not that investing is expensive or requires large amounts of money. Young people spend hundreds of Rands every week on alcohol, smoking, entertainment, and gambling. Affordability is not the issue. The issue is a lack of education, direction, and access to simple, accessible investment products.

We are not taught how to build wealth. Not in schools. Not by parents who themselves were never taught.

Your school taught you trigonometry. I'm still waiting to use it. But compound interest? That would have changed my life. Funny how that works.

Without education, people fall for scams. Pyramid schemes and crypto scams flourish because they offer a false promise of wealth to a population hungry for a better future but starved of credible, easy-to-understand investment solutions. They promise you'll get rich overnight. All you have to do is recruit your mother, your uncle, and that neighbour who owes you money.

This has to change.

That is why I wrote this book. To ask the question nobody seems to be asking:

Why are we so good at selling gambling but so terrible at selling investing?

I want to promote the building of discretionary wealth in every South African home, not just a reliance on employer retirement funds that are rigid and inaccessible when you need them.

I want to see accessible investment products offered by mass-market banks, large retailers, and telecommunications companies. Imagine walking into Shoprite and seeing a "Build Your Future" stand. Imagine your banking app popping up a message about your investment, instead of just showing that the Lotto draw is now R100 million without telling you that your chance of winning is almost zero.

The R100 Investor is built on a simple but powerful idea:

You do not have to be rich to start building wealth. You simply have to start.

You do not need thousands of Rands. You do not need to understand complicated financial jargon. You do not need to predict the stock market. You do not need to wait until you have "made it."

What you need is a plan, discipline, patience, and the willingness to take one small step after another. This book provides the plan. You need to bring your discipline, your patience and your willingness to build wealth.

This book is not about getting rich quickly. It will not teach you how to trade cryptocurrencies, identify the next Naspers or Capitec, or turn R100 into a million Rands overnight. There are enough people selling those dreams already. They're usually driving rented cars and using fake screenshots.

Instead, this book is about something far more important: building a financial life that is resilient, sustainable, and capable of growing over time.

So what does actual investing look like? Not the gambling they're selling you. The real thing. The boring thing. The thing that works.

At its heart is an investment plan known as the Permanent Portfolio—a strategy designed not around predicting the future, but around accepting that none of us can know what the future holds. Rather than trying to guess what comes next, it prepares for many possibilities by combining different types of assets that thrive under different economic conditions.

It is elegant in its simplicity. Prosperity will not last forever. Recessions will happen. Inflation is always present, while deflation is a possibility. Markets will rise and fall. Yet through all of these seasons, disciplined investors who continue to save, diversify, and remain patient allow themselves not merely to survive, but to prosper.

Most importantly, this book speaks directly to

young South Africans.

Whether you are a university student receiving a small allowance, a graduate starting your first job, an entrepreneur building a side hustle, an apprentice learning a trade, or someone still searching for stable employment, the principles in these pages apply to you.

One person may start with R100 a month. Another may invest R500. Someone else may contribute R1,000 or more.

What matters is not where you begin.

What matters is that you begin.

If you develop the habit of investing while you are young, you give yourself something incredibly valuable: TIME. Time allows small contributions to compound. Time allows mistakes to become lessons rather than disasters.

By picking up this book, you have already taken the first step. You have chosen curiosity over complacency. Action over excuses. Hope over helplessness.

The journey to wealth is rarely dramatic. More often, it is quiet. It consists of ordinary decisions repeated month after month: spending a little less than you earn, investing regularly, ignoring distractions, staying diversified, and continuing even when progress feels slow.

There will be setbacks. There will be seasons of doubt. There will be moments when others appear to be getting rich faster through speculation and shortcuts. They'll post about their "massive gains" on Instagram. Don't believe them.

Stay the course.

Real wealth is not built in a day. It is built through habits. It is built through discipline. It is built one month at a time.

Perhaps, years from now, you will look back on this book and realise that the most important lesson was never about shares, bonds, cash, or gold.

It was that you discovered your future does not have to be decided by your circumstances today.

You have more control than you think.

And the journey can begin with something as small as your first R100.

Welcome to your journey.

Turn the page. Your future self is already thanking you.

Senzo Hlangu

Foreword Challenge: Open your banking app right now. Find the Lotto section. Notice how easy it is to gamble. Then close it. Open an EasyEquities account instead. That one action is the difference between being a consumer and becoming an investor.

INTRODUCTION: YOU DON'T NEED TO BE RICH TO START INVESTING

Let me guess what you think an investor looks like.

A man in an expensive suit. A glass office in Sandton. A family that inherited money. Someone who understands complicated financial words you have never heard of.

That's what I thought too. When I was young, investing felt like a club I was never invited to join. There was a bouncer at the door: "Sorry, your name's not on the list. Come back when your salary has more zeros."

Here's the truth I wish someone had told me thirty years ago:

There is no bouncer.

There is no list.

The door is open.

You can walk through it with whatever you have, right now, today.

The Question Nobody Asks

When I meet young South Africans, they usually ask me the same question:

"How much money do I need to start investing?"

They ask it like there's a minimum amount. Like the first R100 isn't enough. Like they need to save up and wait.

That question is wrong.

The real question is:

"What habit do I need to start today?"

Because here's the secret nobody tells you:

The amount you start with doesn't matter.

The habit matters.

R100 invested consistently for forty years becomes a significant sum.

R100 every month for forty years at 10% growth becomes more than R632,000.

You are not too late. You are not too poor. You are not too young.

You are exactly where you need to be.

Three Things You Need to Know

Before we go any further, I need to be honest with you about three things.

First: This book will not make you rich quickly.

There are plenty of books and YouTube videos that promise exactly that.

They are lying.

If someone had a formula for turning R100 into a million Rands overnight, they would be on a beach in Clifton, not writing a book or making videos.

Second: This book is not about gambling.

I won't teach you to trade cryptocurrencies from your bedroom. I won't tell you to buy the next Naspers or Capitec. I won't show you how to become a day trader.

People do become wealthy quickly. There are also people who lose everything trying. They just don't post that part on Instagram.

Third: This book is about doing the boring thing.

The thing that works.

The thing that ordinary people have used for decades to build real wealth.

The thing that doesn't require you to be clever or lucky or well-connected.

Following a credible investment plan. The Permanent Portfolio.

Who This Book Is For

This book is written for young South Africans who want a better financial future, even if they are starting with very little.

It is for:

- The university student receiving a small allowance
- The graduate starting their first job
- The apprentice learning a trade
- The entrepreneur building a side hustle
- The young professional trying to balance rent, transport, and family responsibilities
- The person supporting parents, siblings, or extended family

- The individual who has never invested before but wants to learn

If you have ever thought, "I wish someone had taught me this earlier," this book is for you.

It does not matter whether you can invest R100, R500, or R1,000 each month. The principles remain the same.

What matters is developing the mindset and habits that allow wealth to grow over time.

What This Book Is Not

This book is not a promise of overnight riches.

It is not about becoming wealthy by next month.

It is not a guide to day trading, gambling on the latest market craze, or chasing the next "guaranteed" investment opportunity.

You will not find secret formulas that promise to turn R100 into a million Rands overnight. If I had that formula, I'd be on a beach in Clifton, not writing books.

You will not be encouraged to take unnecessary risks.

You will not be taught to speculate based on rumours, social media trends, or fear of missing out.

There are people who become wealthy quickly. There are also many people who lose everything trying. They just don't post that part on Facebook or Instagram.

This book takes a different approach.

It focuses on building wealth slowly, steadily, and responsibly.

It values discipline over excitement. Consistency over prediction. Preparation over speculation.

Because staying in the game is often more important than trying to win it all at once.

Why Simple Beats Complicated

Many people assume that successful investing must be complicated.

The financial industry often reinforces this belief through technical language, complex products, and endless predictions about what will happen next.

But complexity does not always lead to better outcomes.

In fact, complexity often leads to confusion.

Confusion leads to inaction. Or worse, expensive mistakes.

Simple strategies are easier to understand.

They are easier to stick with when markets become volatile.

They reduce the temptation to constantly change direction.

They help ordinary people make good decisions consistently.

The strategy you will learn in this book is simple by design.

It recognises a powerful truth: nobody can predict the future with certainty. Not even that economist you regularly see on TV knows exactly when the Rand would weaken.

No one knows exactly when the next recession will arrive.

No one knows when inflation will surge.

No one knows which investment will be the best performer next year.

Instead of trying to predict the future, you can

prepare for it.

Simple does not mean simplistic.

Simple means practical. Simple means understandable. Simple means sustainable.

And sustainable habits are often what separate successful investors from everyone else.

How to Get the Most from This Guide

You do not need to read this book in one sitting.

Take your time.

Reflect on the ideas.

Discuss them with friends and family.

Ask questions.

Challenge assumptions.

Most importantly, take action and begin investing.

As you read:

- Focus on understanding the principles rather than memorising facts
- Resist the temptation to skip ahead looking for shortcuts

- Remember that investing is a lifelong journey, not a once-off event
- Start applying what you learn, even in small ways
- Do not wait until you feel completely ready

No investor begins with perfect knowledge.

Every experienced investor was once a beginner.

Every large portfolio started small.

Every journey started with a first step.

By the time you finish this book,

- you will understand why investing matters,
- how to protect and grow your wealth through different economic seasons, and
- how to build a simple investment strategy suited to ordinary South Africans.

But knowledge alone is not enough.

The goal is not merely to understand investing.

The goal is to become an investor.

And perhaps your journey begins today—with your first R100.

Key Takeaways

- You don't need to be rich to start investing—the habit matters more than the amount
- The real question is not "How much money do I need?" but "What habit do I need to start today?"
- This book will not make you rich quickly—it focuses on building wealth slowly, steadily, and responsibly
- Simple strategies beat complicated ones because they are easier to understand and stick with
- The goal is not merely to understand investing—the goal is to become an investor
- Start with whatever you have, right where you are

Try This Today

1. Open your banking app

2. Find your expenses from the last month
3. Find ONE thing you can cut (not everything—just one thing)
4. Transfer R100 to a separate savings account
5. Write on a piece of paper: **"This is my first investment."**

Done. You are no longer someone who reads about investing. You are an investor.

Did You Know?

R100 invested every month for 40 years at 10% growth becomes more than R630,000. R100 spent every month for 40 years becomes memories and receipts. The choice is yours.

Reflection from the Stoics

The Stoics teach that we suffer more from our imagination than from reality. The fear of investing—the fear of losing money, of making a mistake, of looking foolish—is often far worse than the actual experience.

What if you treated your first R100 not as a gamble, but as an experiment in self-discipline?

What if the goal was not to get rich, but to prove to yourself that you can keep a promise to your future self?

Start small but start. The act of beginning is a declaration that you refuse to let fear decide your future.

What You've Learned So Far

Chapter	Key Lesson
Introduction	You don't need to be rich to start. The habit matters more than the amount.

What's Next

In Chapter 1, we'll explore why working hard is not enough.

You will learn:

- Why the old promise of "work hard, retire comfortably" no longer holds true
- How the salary trap keeps you running in place
- The invisible thief that steals from savers every day
- Why most people never start investing—and how to be different

The next chapter is about understanding the problem so you can solve it.

CHAPTER 1: WHY WORKING HARD IS NOT ENOUGH

"If a man knows not to which port he sails, no wind is favourable." — Seneca

The Promise

Remember the promise?

"Study hard. Get good grades. Find a stable job. Work hard. Climb the ladder. Save what you can. Retire comfortably."

It was the promise your parents believed. Your teachers reinforced. Society repeated like a mantra.

Work hard. Be responsible. Everything will work out.

It was a beautiful promise.

It was also a lie.

Think about your parents' generation.

When they entered the workforce, things were different. Jobs came with pensions. Staying with one employer for thirty years was normal—these days, staying with one employer for 10 years feels like a lifetime achievement award.

The cost of housing, education, and healthcare was closer to what salaries could actually buy.

That world is gone.

Today, young South Africans face something different. Permanent jobs are harder to find than a seat on a taxi at 5pm. Wages haven't kept up with the cost of basic necessities. The safety nets that protected previous generations have frayed or disappeared.

And yet, we keep following the old playbook.

Work hard. Show up on time. Take on extra responsibility. Hope for promotions that might never come. Save what little remains. Wonder why progress feels so slow—like trying to accelerate with the handbrake on.

The uncomfortable truth is this:

Working hard is necessary.

But it is not enough.

The Salary Trap

Here's something that will mess with your head.

Imagine two friends.

Thabo earns R25,000 a month. He pays R10,000 for rent and transport. He has R15,000 left. He uses it to improve his lifestyle. Better food. A nicer phone. Nicer clothes. Weekend trips. At the end of the month, little remains.

Lerato earns R25,000 a month. She pays R10,000 for rent and transport. She has R15,000 left. She lives as if she still earns R15,000. She invests R10,000 a month.

After ten years, assuming reasonable returns, Lerato has built a substantial portfolio.

Thabo has a wardrobe of clothes now out of fashion and a phone that's already been replaced by a newer model.

Both worked hard. Both earned the same.

One built wealth. The other built stuff.

This is the salary trap.

When you earn more, you spend more. Not because you're irresponsible. Because life gets more expensive in ways that are hard to avoid.

A promotion might mean a reliable car for a longer commute. A better job might mean professional clothes or more education. A safer neighbourhood means more rent. More responsibility means less time to cook at home.

This is sometimes called lifestyle creep.

In South Africa, we call it: **"The moment you upgrade from amagwinya with polony to sushi and wonder where your salary went."**

The problem is not the size of your salary.

The problem is that salaries are linear and life is complex.

You trade time for money. But there are only twenty-four hours in a day. You can only get so many promotions. You can only climb so high before you hit a ceiling.

And even if you reach that ceiling, unexpected events—illness, retrenchment, family emergencies—can undo years of progress in weeks.

Relying solely on earned income is risky because earned income stops the moment you stop working.

Building wealth requires something that salaries alone cannot provide:

Assets that work while you sleep.

The Invisible Thief

There's a second problem.

Everything gets more expensive over time.

A loaf of bread that cost R5 a decade ago now costs R15. A litre of petrol that was R12 is now R25. Electricity tariffs increase faster than most salaries—you pay more for the privilege of sitting in the dark during load shedding. Rent. Medical aid. School fees. Transport. All climb upward.

This is inflation.

When inflation is higher than your salary increase, you are taking a pay cut even when your payslip shows a higher number.

Between 2010 and 2025, South Africa experienced cumulative inflation of more than 100%. That means something costing R100 in 2010 required more than R200 to buy in 2025.

If your salary did not more than double during that period, you lost ground even while working hard. You ran a marathon and ended up behind the starting line.

Inflation does not care how many hours you

work. It does not care about your dedication. It does not care about your qualifications. It simply erodes the value of idle money.

This is why keeping all your money in a bank account is a losing strategy.

You are running as fast as you can just to stay in the same place.

The Real Cost of "I'll Start Investing Next Year"

There is a cost to waiting that most people never calculate.

Every year you delay investing, you lose twice:

1. You lose the contributions you didn't make
2. You lose the compounding those contributions would have earned

Let me show you what this actually means.

Thabo decides to wait. He wants to clear his debt first. Then build an emergency fund. Then save for a deposit on a car. He plans to start investing at 30. It sounds responsible.

Lerato decides to start immediately. She invests R500 per month from age 25.

Both invest R500 per month until age 65. Both earn the same return.

But Thabo lost five years of compounding.

At age 65, Lerato has substantially more. The five-year delay cost Thabo hundreds of thousands of Rands in potential wealth.

This is not because Thabo did anything wrong. It is because inflation and compounding work together in two different ways:

- Compounding rewards early starters
- Inflation punishes late starters

The hidden cost of waiting is the largest expense most young investors will ever face.

And unlike bank fees or transaction costs, this expense is invisible. You can't see it on any statement. You only feel it years later when you realise how far behind you are.

The Unemployment Reality

Not everyone reading this book has a job.

South Africa's unemployment rate, particularly among young people, is among the highest in the world. More than half of young South Africans are not employed. Graduates struggle to find entry-level positions. Experienced professionals face retrenchments as companies restructure.

For those without a steady salary, the idea of investing can seem laughable—like offering someone a gym membership while they're trying to find their next meal.

How can you invest when you cannot afford rent? How can you think about the future when survival consumes today?

These are fair questions.

But the principles in this book still apply, even in difficult circumstances.

When income is uncertain or non-existent, the focus shifts to three things:

1. **Building skills** that increase earning potential over time. Your ability to earn is your most valuable asset.
2. **Reducing expenses** to their absolute minimum. Every Rand saved is a Rand that does not need to be earned.
3. **Starting as small as possible** once some stability returns. Even R50 per month establishes the habit.

The goal is not to pretend unemployment does not exist. The goal is to prepare for the day when income returns, so that you do not waste years trying to catch up.

Side Hustles and Irregular Income

Many young South Africans have embraced side hustles.

Driving for delivery services. Selling goods online. Freelancing skills. Tutoring. Creative work. Consulting. Spaza shops. Building small businesses alongside formal employment or in place of it.

This is a rational response to an economy that no longer offers stable, single-employer careers.

But side hustles come with their own challenges. Income is often irregular. One month you might earn R5,000 extra. The next month, nothing. This unpredictability makes traditional investing advice—"invest 10 percent of your salary each month"—difficult to apply.

The solution is to think in terms of averages rather than fixed amounts.

If you earn R3,000 from your side hustle in January and R0 in February, your average over two months is R1,500. You can aim to invest a percentage of that average, investing more in good months and nothing in lean months.

The habit matters more than the consistency of the amount.

What destroys progress is not investing in lean months.

What destroys progress is stopping entirely.

The Fees You Can't See

The financial industry is not always your friend.

Banks charge monthly fees. Investment products come with hidden costs. Insurance policies include commissions that enrich salespeople—sometimes they're selling you a product like a waiter pushing the most expensive wine on the menu.

These fees might seem small. One percent here. Half a percent there.

But over decades, fees compound just like returns do—just in the wrong direction.

High fees can consume a third or more of your potential growth. You work hard to earn money. You invest it carefully. And then fees quietly steal from your future, like a friend who always "forgets" their wallet when the bill arrives.

This book emphasises low-cost investment vehicles like exchange-traded funds (ETFs) for

exactly this reason.

Keeping costs low is one of the few things within your control that reliably improves outcomes.

Why Most People Never Start

Most people never start investing for reasons that have nothing to do with their bank balance.

- They do not start because investing feels complicated
- They do not start because they are afraid of making mistakes
- They do not start because they believe they need more money first
- They do not start because no one ever showed them how
- They do not start because they assume it is too late
- They do not start because they are waiting for the perfect moment

The perfect moment never arrives.

Like pothole-free roads across South Africa, it's a beautiful dream but not something to build your life around.

There will always be a reason to delay. A debt to pay first. A family obligation. An unexpected expense. A better time that is always just ahead.

Years pass. The habit never forms. The money that could have been growing sits idle or is spent. The opportunity cost becomes enormous.

This is the quiet tragedy of personal finance.

Not the people who try and fail.

The people who never try at all.

The Good News

After reading all of this, you might feel discouraged.

Working hard is not enough. Salaries are a trap. Inflation is eating your money. Unemployment is high. Side hustles are uncertain. Fees are everywhere. Fear is paralyzing.

Where is the hope?

The hope is that you now understand the problem. And understanding the problem is the first step toward solving it.

As Epictetus put it: "First say to yourself what you would be; and then do what you have to do."

The good news is this:

- You do not need to predict the future

- You do not need to beat the market
- You do not need a finance or economics degree
- You do not need a large salary
- You do not need perfect timing

What you need is a simple, proven investment strategy that works across different economic conditions.

A strategy that protects you from inflation, recession, and uncertainty.

A strategy that allows you to start small and grow steadily.

A strategy that ordinary people have used for decades to build real wealth.

That strategy is the Permanent Portfolio.

In the next chapter, we'll meet inflation face to face—and understand exactly why doing nothing is the most dangerous choice you can make.

But for now, remember:

Working hard is not enough.

But working hard while investing consistently is a powerful combination.

You don't have to choose between earning income and building wealth.

You can do both.

And you can start with whatever you have, right where you are.

Key Takeaways

- The old promise that hard work alone guarantees financial security no longer holds true in today's economy
- Earning more only builds wealth if you keep the gap between income and expenses wide enough to invest consistently
- Inflation silently erodes purchasing power, punishing those who rely entirely on earned income and cash savings
- Most people never start investing because of fear, confusion, or waiting for the perfect moment—not because they lack money
- The good news is that a simple, disciplined investment strategy exists that works for ordinary people starting with small amounts
- **You can start today with whatever you have, right where you are**

Try This Today

1. Open your banking app
2. Look at your expenses from the last month
3. Find ONE thing you can cut (not everything—just one thing)
4. Transfer that amount to a separate savings account
5. Write down: **"This is my first investment. I am now an investor."**

Did You Know?

- R100 invested every month for 40 years at 10% growth becomes more than R630,000
- R100 spent every month for 40 years becomes memories and receipts
- The choice is yours

Reflection from the Stoics

Marcus Aurelius reminded himself each morning that he would meet people who were meddling, ungrateful, arrogant, dishonest, jealous, and surly—and that he should not be surprised, because that is simply the nature of human beings.

The economy is no different.

It will be unstable, unpredictable, and often unfair. Expecting it to be otherwise is the root of frustration.

Your task is not to complain about inflation, unemployment, or broken promises.

Your task is to build a personal system that can withstand all of those things.

When you accept that the economy owes you nothing, you become free to build something it cannot take away.

What You've Learned So Far

Chapter	Key Lesson
Introduction	You don't need to be rich to start. The habit matters more than the amount.
Chapter 1	Working hard is not enough. You need assets that work while you sleep.

What's Next

In Chapter 2, we'll meet the thief in your pocket.

You will learn:

- What inflation really is and how it steals from you every day
- Why saving money in a bank account is not as safe as you think
- How everyday expenses like food, transport, and electricity are killing your budget
- The hidden cost of waiting to invest

The next chapter will show you exactly what you're up against—and why doing nothing is the most dangerous choice you can make.

CHAPTER 2: THE THIEF IN YOUR POCKET

Inflation: The Invisible Enemy

"He who is not contented with what he has, would not be contented with what he would like to have." — Epictetus

The Grandmother's Lesson

Let me tell you about my grandmother.

She was careful with money. Frugal. Disciplined. Everything we were told to be.

For twenty years, she put aside whatever she could. R50 here. R100 there. From her pension grant. From the vegetables she grew in her backyard and sold to neighbours. From money sent by her children working in the cities.

She didn't spend it. She didn't lose it. She didn't give

it away.

She saved it.

By the time she died, she had R35,000 in her savings account.

She thought she had built a fortune.

In 2000, R35,000 could buy a small car. Or pay a year's university fees. Or serve as a deposit on a modest house.

By the time she died, R35,000 could cover three months of expenses.

My grandmother had been careful for two decades.

She had done everything right.

And inflation had stolen most of it.

Meet the Thief

Imagine someone entered your home while you slept.

They didn't break a window. They didn't pick a lock. They left no fingerprints. They made no noise. They stole a small portion of everything you own.

And they come back every single day.

Taking a little more. Not enough to notice immediately. But enough that over months and years, the loss becomes enormous.

This thief exists.

Its name is inflation.

Inflation is the gradual increase in prices across an economy. As prices rise, each Rand buys a little less than it did yesterday.

A loaf of bread costs more. A tank of petrol costs more. Rent costs more. School fees cost more. Electricity costs more.

Everything costs more.

The cruelest part?

Inflation punishes the very behaviour most people believe is responsible:

Saving money in a bank account.

You work hard. You spend less than you earn. You put the difference aside for the future. You are doing everything right.

And inflation slowly steals from you anyway.

This is why understanding inflation is the first and most important step toward becoming a successful investor.

If you do not understand inflation, you will make poor decisions. You will keep too much money in cash. You will delay investing. You will watch your purchasing power shrink year after year while believing you are being careful.

The good news is that once you understand inflation, you can protect yourself against it.

But first, you need to see the thief clearly.

What R100 Used to Buy

Let me show you what inflation actually does.

In 2000, a R100 note could buy approximately:

- 20 loaves of bread
- 10 litres of petrol
- A full week of groceries for one person

By 2025, that same R100 note couldn't buy a single one of those things.

The note looks the same. The number printed on it is unchanged.

But its power has been destroyed.

This is not a mystery. It is not bad luck. It is simply how modern economies work.

When a central bank like the South African Reserve Bank increases the supply of money faster than the production of goods and services, prices rise.

The South African Reserve Bank tries to manage inflation, keeping it within a target range of 3 to 6 percent.

But even at the lower end of that range, inflation cuts your purchasing power in half approximately every fifteen years.

If inflation averages 6 percent, your money loses half its value in just twelve years.

Think about that.

If you keep R100,000 in a bank account earning negligible interest, in twelve years it will buy what R50,000 buys today.

You have lost R50,000 of purchasing power without spending a single cent.

This is why saving alone is not enough.

You must invest.

Why Food, Transport, and Electricity Are Killing Your Budget

Inflation is not an abstract economic concept. You experience it every time you visit a shop, fill up your car, or pay your bills.

In South Africa, you experience it when you look at the price of a simple pie at a petrol station. (Remember when a pie was R10? Now it's R25. And it's smaller.)

Let's look at the numbers.

Bread

In 2010, a standard loaf of brown bread cost around R6.

By 2015, it had risen to approximately R9.

By 2020, around R12.

By 2025, many loaves cost R16 or more.

If you eat one loaf a week, you're spending an extra R500 a year in 2025 compared to 2010, just on bread.

That R500 could have been invested.

Petrol

In 2010, a litre of petrol averaged around R8.

By 2015, it had climbed past R12.

By 2020, it fluctuated between R14 and R17.

By 2025, prices regularly exceeded R25 per litre.

If you commute 40 kilometres per day in a fuel-efficient car, your monthly petrol expense rose from approximately R500 to more than R1,500.

At this rate, you'll soon need a second job just to afford the drive to the first one.

Electricity

This is perhaps the most painful example.

Between 2010 and 2025, electricity prices rose by more than 400%.

A household paying R400 per month for electricity in 2010 found themselves paying more than R2,000 per month by 2025.

That's paying more for the privilege of sitting in the dark during load shedding.

These are not luxuries. These are basics.

Food. Transport. Electricity. The things you cannot live without.

If your salary did not increase by at least the same percentage as these costs, you are worse off today than you were years ago.

You are working just as hard, but you can afford less.

Your standard of living has been reduced.

And you did nothing wrong.

The Declining Power of the Rand

Let's look at the numbers more directly.

According to Statistics South Africa, the cumulative inflation rate between 2010 and 2025 exceeded 100%.

Some years were worse than others, but the trend was consistently upward. There was hardly any time when prices fell and the purchasing power of our money increased.

Prices always go up.

Always.

What does this mean in practical terms?

If you earned R10,000 per month in 2010, you needed to earn more than R20,000 per month in 2025 just to maintain the same standard of living.

Not to get ahead. Not to build wealth.

Just to stay exactly where you were.

It's like running on a treadmill that keeps speeding up.

Many salaries did not keep pace.

The average real wage in South Africa—meaning wages adjusted for inflation—has grown very slowly over the past two decades. Some sectors have seen declines.

Many workers have lost purchasing power even as their nominal salaries increased.

The Two Friends

Consider two friends who graduated together in 2010.

Themba started investing immediately, putting R500 per month into a diversified portfolio that grew faster than inflation.

Sandile also put R500 per month, but in a bank account earning 2% interest while inflation averaged 5%.

By 2025:

- Themba A had built real wealth. Their money had grown substantially above inflation.
- Sandile had lost purchasing power despite saving diligently. Their R500 per month had been eaten away year after year.

Both worked hard. Both saved.

But only one understood inflation well enough to protect themselves.

Why Savers Lose When They Do Nothing

There is a common belief that saving money is always good and always safe.

Saving is good.

But saving in the wrong way is not safe.

It's like storing your drinking water in a leaky bucket. You're doing the right thing, but the container is betraying you.

If you store your money under a mattress, inflation steals from you every single day.

If you keep your money in a standard savings account earning 1 or 2% interest while inflation runs at 5 or 6%, you lose 3 to 4% of your purchasing power each year.

This is not safety.

This is slow, predictable, and guaranteed loss.

Many people choose savings accounts because they are terrified of losing money in the stock market. But they do not realise that they are choosing a different kind of loss:

The certain and permanent loss of purchasing power over time.

Let me show you what this actually looks like.

What Happens to R10,000 in a Savings Account

Years	2% Interest, 5% Inflation	What Your R10,000 Can Actually Buy
0	R10,000 in bank	R10,000
5	Interest earned, inflation steals	R8,500 in buying power
10	Interest earned, inflation steals	R7,000
15	Interest earned, inflation steals	R5,500
20	Interest earned, inflation steals	R4,000

After twenty years, your careful savings have lost more than half their purchasing power.

You have done everything society told you to do. You worked hard. You saved. You avoided risk.

And you have less than you started with.

This is why doing nothing is not a neutral choice.

Doing nothing is choosing to lose.

The Hidden Cost of Waiting

Beyond the direct loss from inflation, there is another cost that is harder to see but equally damaging:

The cost of waiting.

Every year you delay investing is a year that inflation eats away at your money while also robbing you of potential growth.

Let me show you what this looks like.

Thabo and Nonhlanhla

Thabo and Nonhlanhla are both 25 years old.

Thabo decides to wait.

He wants to clear his debt first. Then he wants to build an emergency fund. Then he wants to save for a deposit on a car. He plans to start investing at age 30.

It's a responsible-sounding plan—the financial equivalent of "I'll start going to gym in January."

Nonhlanhla decides to start immediately.

She invests R500 per month from age 25. She invests consistently until age 65.

Both invest R500 per month until age 65. Both earn the same inflation-beating return.

But Thabo lost five years of compounding.

At age 65, Nonhlanhla has accumulated substantially more than Thabo.

The five-year delay cost Thabo hundreds of thousands of Rands in potential wealth.

This is not because Thabo did anything wrong.

It is because inflation and compounding work together in two different ways:

- Compounding rewards early starters
- Inflation punishes late starters

Every year you wait, you lose twice:

1. Once to inflation eating your idle cash
2. Once to the missed growth that money could have earned

The hidden cost of waiting is the largest expense most young investors will ever face.

And unlike bank fees or transaction costs, this expense is invisible. You cannot see it on any statement. You only feel it years later when you realise how far behind you are.

The Zimbabwe Lesson

Want to see what happens when you ignore inflation?

Look at our neighbours in Zimbabwe.

At one point, the Zimbabwean dollar collapsed so badly that people needed a wheelbarrow full of cash to buy a loaf of bread.

Banknotes became wallpaper. Life savings became worthless overnight.

The people who survived?

Those who owned hard assets. Property. Foreign currency. And gold.

South Africa is not Zimbabwe.

Our institutions are stronger. Our currency has not collapsed.

But the same forces exist. The same temptation to print money. The same erosion of purchasing power.

And the same lesson:

You cannot rely on the currency alone to protect your wealth.

Protecting Your Future Self

By now, you might feel alarmed.

Good.

A little alarm is appropriate. Inflation is a serious threat to your financial future. Pretending it does not exist will not protect you.

But alarm without action is just anxiety.

The purpose of understanding inflation is not to frighten you. The purpose is to motivate you to take action.

You protect yourself from inflation by owning assets that tend to increase in value when prices rise.

Different assets perform differently during inflationary periods.

Asset	How It Performs During Inflation
Cash	Loses value

Fixed-interest bonds	Loses value
Equities (shares)	Tends to hold or increase value
Property	Tends to hold or increase value
Gold	Tends to hold or increase value

The Permanent Portfolio strategy you will learn in this book includes assets specifically chosen to protect you during different economic conditions—including periods of high inflation.

You do not need to predict when inflation will rise or fall. You simply need to own a diversified mix of assets that together protect you across all economic seasons.

This is the beauty of the approach.

You cannot stop inflation.

You cannot avoid it.

You can only prepare for it.

And preparation begins with a single decision:

To stop letting inflation steal from you while you wait for a perfect moment that will never arrive.

Your future self will thank you for starting today.

Because the thief is already inside your home.

Every day you delay, it takes a little more.

The only question is whether you will continue to let it steal from you—or whether you will fight back.

Real Numbers: What Inflation Has Done to the Rand

Year	What R100 Could Buy	Equivalent in 2025
2000	40 loaves of bread	R250+
2005	30 loaves of bread	R200
2010	25 litres of petrol	R190
2015	20 litres of petrol	R160
2020	15 litres of petrol	R130
2025	8 litres of petrol	R100

The Rand has lost more than half its purchasing power in 25 years.

And it will keep losing.

The only question is whether you will let it steal your purchasing power.

What Young South Africans Need to Know

The education system won't teach you this.

My school taught me trigonometry. I'm still waiting to use it.

But compound interest? Inflation? Investing?

That would have changed my life.

Your parents might not know this.

They were taught the same things you were. Work hard. Save. Be responsible.

They didn't know about the invisible thief.

The financial industry won't tell you this.

They make money from complexity. From fear. From convincing you that investing is too hard for ordinary people.

Now you know.

And knowing is the first step to doing.

Common Myths About Inflation

Myth: "Inflation doesn't affect me. I don't own much."

Fact: Inflation affects everyone who uses money. If you buy food, pay rent, or use transport, inflation affects you. The less you own, the more inflation hurts.

Myth: "I have a savings account. I'm safe."

Fact: A savings account that earns less than inflation is a slow leak in your life raft. You are losing purchasing power every day.

Myth: "I'll start investing when I earn more."

Fact: If you can't invest with a small amount, you won't invest with a large amount. The habit must come first. The amount can grow later.

Myth: "Inflation will come down eventually."

Fact: Inflation never goes away completely. It might slow down. It might speed up. But it never stops entirely. **You need a permanent solution.**

Key Takeaways

- Inflation is a hidden thief that slowly steals your money's purchasing power over time
- At 5-6% inflation, your money loses half its value in approximately twelve to fifteen years
- Everyday expenses like food, transport, and electricity have risen much faster than many salaries
- Keeping money in bank accounts guarantees a slow, predictable, and permanent loss of purchasing power
- Waiting to invest has a hidden double cost: inflation eats your cash while you miss out

on potential growth

- You cannot stop inflation, but you can protect yourself by owning assets that tend to hold or increase their value during inflationary periods
- The Permanent Portfolio includes assets specifically chosen to guard against inflation while also protecting you during other economic conditions

Try This Today

1. Go to your bank's savings account. Look at the interest rate.
2. Now Google "South Africa inflation rate."
3. If your interest rate is lower than inflation (it almost certainly is), write this number on a piece of paper: **"X% loss every year."** That's the cost of doing nothing.
4. Now look at your phone. Open your banking app. Notice how easy it is to gamble. Notice how hard it is to invest.

Ask yourself: "What am I going to do about it?"

Answer: "Start today."

Did You Know?

A R100 note from 2000 would buy 40 loaves of bread. Today, it buys 8.

At 6% inflation, your money loses half its value in 12 years.

South Africa's inflation rate has exceeded 5% for most of the past two decades.

If you are not investing, you are losing.

Reflection from the Stoics

The Stoic philosopher Epictetus taught that we should concern ourselves only with what is in our power.

Inflation is not in your power.

The Reserve Bank's policies are not in your power.

The global price of oil is not in your power.

But your response is entirely within your power.

Where you place your savings. How you allocate your resources. Whether you choose to act or remain passive.

When you stop worrying about the thief you cannot catch and start building walls it cannot easily climb, you reclaim your power.

Do not waste energy resenting inflation.

Use that energy to outsmart it.

What You've Learned So Far

Chapter	Key Lesson

Intro-duction	You don't need to be rich to start. The habit matters more than the amount.
Chapter 1	Working hard is not enough. You need assets that work while you sleep.
Chapter 2	Inflation is the invisible thief. It steals from savers every day.

You now understand the problem.

Your Challenge

Before you read the next chapter:

1. Open your banking app.
2. Find a savings account.
3. Check the interest rate.
4. Google the current inflation rate.
5. Calculate the difference.
6. **Ask yourself: "Am I losing money without knowing it?"**
7. **Commit to doing something about it.**

You are no longer someone who doesn't know about inflation.

You now know.

And knowing means you can act.

What's Next

In Chapter 3, we'll discover why being young is your greatest advantage.

You will learn:

- The magic of compounding and why time is your superpower
- What R100 a month can become over 40 years
- The cost of waiting
- Why starting early is the single most powerful thing you can do

The next chapter will show you that your age is not a disadvantage—it's your greatest asset.

CHAPTER 3: WHY BEING YOUNG IS YOUR GREATEST ADVANTAGE

Time Is Your Superpower

"No great thing is created suddenly." — Epictetus

The 25-Year-Old Who Became a Millionaire

Let me tell you about Sipho.

Sipho was 25 years old. He worked as an apprentice electrician. He earned a modest salary. He didn't have a fancy car. He didn't have a degree. He didn't inherit money.

But Sipho started investing.

He committed R500 a month. Not a huge amount.

The equivalent of a few trips to shisanyama, two cases of beer, a couple of taxi trips, one night out.

He invested that R500 every month, without fail, for 40 years.

He didn't increase his contributions. He didn't try to time the market. He didn't chase hot tips.

He just invested. Consistently. Relentlessly.

At age 65, Sipho had invested a total of R 240,000.

His portfolio was worth approximately R 3.1 million.

Sipho started with nothing.

He invested the equivalent of two cases of beer per month.

He became a millionaire.

The Cost of Waiting

Now let me tell you about Lerato.

Lerato was also 25. She also earned a modest salary. She also wanted to invest.

But Lerato decided to wait.

"I need to clear my debt first."

"I need to build an emergency fund."

"I'll start when I earn more."

"I'll start next year."

Next year came. And went. And came again.

Finally, at age 30, Lerato started investing R 500 a month.

She invested for 35 years instead of 40.

By age 65, Lerato had invested a total of R 210,000.

Her portfolio was worth approximately R 1,9 mil.

By starting just five years earlier, Sipho ended up with R 1,2 mil more than Lerato, even though he invested only R 30,000 more than Lerato.

Five years of delay.

R 1,2 mil of lost wealth.

That's R 240,000 per year of procrastination.

The Even Higher Cost

Now let me tell you about Jabu.

Jabu was 35. She had worked for a decade but never invested. "I always meant to," she said. "But life got in the way."

She finally started at 35. R500 a month. Until age 65.

She invested for 30 years. Her total contributions were R180,000.

At age 65, her portfolio was worth approximately R 1.1 mil.

Compared to Sipho, Jabu ended up with R 2 mil less, even though she invested only R 60,000 less than Sipho.

The ten-year delay cost her R2 million Rands.

That's a 2 to 4 houses in many parts of the country.

Gone. Because of waiting.

The Numbers Don't Lie

Let me show you what this looks like in a table. All investors earn 10% return per year.

Name	Started At	Monthly Investment	Years Invested	Total Invested	Value at 65
Sipho	25	R500	40	R240,000	R3,162,040
Lerato	30	R500	35	R210,000	R1,898,319
Jabu	35	R500	30	R180,000	R1,130,244

Every year you delay costs you more than you think.

Not just the contributions you didn't make.

The compounding those contributions would have earned.

The Magic of Compounding

Compounding means your investment earnings generate their own earnings.

Here's how it works:

Year 1: You invest R1,000. You earn 10% = R100. You have R1,100.

Year 2: You earn 10% on R1,100 = R110. You have R1,210.

Year 3: You earn 10% on R1,210 = R121. You have R1,331.

The extra money isn't just from your contributions. It's from your returns earning returns.

Over short periods, this effect is small.

Over decades, it is enormous.

It's like planting a tree: for the first few years it looks like a stick, and then suddenly it's providing shade for the whole yard.

The Rule of 72

There's a simple rule called the Rule of 72.

It tells you how long it takes for your money to double.

Take 72 and divide it by your expected return.

Expected Return	Years to Double
6%	12 years
7%	10.3 years
8%	9 years
10%	7.2 years

So if you earn 8% per year, your money doubles every 9 years.

Year 0: R1,000

Year 9: R2,000

Year 18: R4,000

Year 27: R8,000

Year 36: R16,000

Your money doesn't just grow.

It grows faster over time.

What R100 a Month Becomes

Let me show you what a small monthly investment can become.

R100 a month for 40 years at 10% growth:

Total invested: R48,000

Final value: Approximately R632,400

R200 a month for 40 years at 10% growth:

Total invested: R96,000

Final value: Approximately R1.2 million

R500 a month for 40 years at 10% growth:

Total invested: R240,000

Final value: Approximately R3.1 million

R1,000 a month for 40 years at 10% growth:

Total invested: R480,000

Final value: Approximately R6.3 million

Small amounts become large amounts.

But only if you start early and stay consistent.

The Cost of Waiting

Let me show you what waiting costs in real terms.

Age You Start	Monthly Invest-ment	Value at 65	Cost of Waiting
25	R500	R3,162,040	Base
30	R500	R1,898,319	-R1,263,721
35	R500	R1,130,244	-R2,031,796
40	R500	R663,417	-R2,498,623

At age 30, the cost of waiting is more that one million Rands.

Age age 35, the cost of has increased to two millions Rands.

This is costly.

Why Young People Have an Unfair Advantage

Young people have something that older investors can never get:

Time.

No matter how rich or how clever they are, older investors cannot buy more time.

But you have time.

You have 40 years. 45 years. Even 50 years.

Time is your superpower.

Use it.

The Emotional Power of Starting Early

Beyond the mathematics, starting early gives you something else:

Confidence.

When you start early, you experience market cycles when your portfolio is small.

You learn to handle crashes when the losses are small.

You learn to rebalance when the stakes are low.

You build the emotional muscles that will serve you when your portfolio is large.

Starting early is not just about compounding.

It's about building the investor mindset.

What Could That Money Do?

R3.1 million could:

Pay off a house

Fund a child's university education

Provide a comfortable retirement

Generate R18,000 a month in sustainable income

Give you the freedom to change careers, start a business, or travel

That's what R500 a month can become.

That's what starting early can do.

The Best Time to Plant a Tree

There's a famous Chinese proverb:

"The best time to plant a tree was 20 years ago. The second-best time is today."

The same is true for investing.

The best time to start was when you were 18.

The second-best time is today.

Not tomorrow.

Not next month.

Not when you have more money.

Today.

Common Myths About Starting

Myth: "I don't have enough money to start."

Fact: You don't need enough. You need the habit.

Start with R100.

Myth: "I'll start when I earn more."

Fact: If you can't start with R100, you won't start with R10,000. The habit must come first.

Myth: "It's too late for me."

Fact: It's never too late. The best time was yesterday. The second-best time is now.

Myth: "I'll miss out if I invest now."

Fact: You'll miss out if you don't. Your money will be eaten by inflation.

The Non-Negotiable Truth

Here's the truth that most people never accept:

You can't get time back.

You can get more money. You can get a better job. You can get a promotion.

But you can't get more time.

Every day you delay investing is a day you can't get back.

That's why starting early is non-negotiable.

If you're 25 and you start today, you will be a millionaire by retirement.

That is almost certain.

If you're 25 and you wait, you will have less.

That is also almost certain.

The choice is yours.

Key Takeaways

- Time is your most powerful advantage. Start as early as possible.
- Compounding means your returns earn returns. Small amounts grow large over decades.
- A five-year delay can cost you hundreds of thousands of Rands in final wealth.
- Every year you wait has a hidden cost that compounds over time.
- Starting early also builds emotional resilience and investor confidence.
- The best time to start was yesterday. The second-best time is today.

Try This Today

1. Open a calculator on your phone
2. Type in R500 × 12 months × 40 years = R240,000
3. That's your total contribution over 40 years
4. Now go to a compound interest calculator online
5. Type in R500 per month, 10% return, 40

years

6. **Watch what happens**
7. **Now imagine what could happen if you started today**

Did You Know?

Warren Buffett made 99% of his wealth after age 50. But he started investing at age 11. His early start gave him decades of compounding. By age 65, he was a billionaire.

His time started early. So can yours.

Reflection from the Stoics

Epictetus said: **"No great thing is created suddenly."**

You don't build a house by laying all the bricks at once.

One brick at a time builds a home.

Wealth begins as R100 a month.

The Stoics valued patience and process over outcomes. You cannot control the market's return, but you can control your consistency.

Time is your ally only if you give it something to work with.

Start small, start now, and let the years do what only years can do.

When you are tempted to feel that you have left it too late, remember:

The best time to plant a tree was twenty years ago.

The second-best time is today.

What You've Learned So Far

Chapter	Key Lesson
Introduction	You don't need to be rich to start. The habit matters more than the amount.
Chapter 1	Working hard is not enough. You need assets that work while you sleep.
Chapter 2	Inflation is the invisible thief. It steals from savers every day.
Chapter 3	Time is your superpower. Start early and let compounding work for you.

What's Next

In Chapter 4, we'll explore the difference between looking rich and being wealthy.

You will learn:

- Why appearances can be deceiving when it comes to wealth
- The difference between permanent loss and temporary decline
- Why liquidity matters more than you think
- Why safety must come before growth

The next chapter is about protecting what you build—because wealth is not just about earning money, it's about keeping it.

CHAPTER 4: LOOKING RICH VS. BEING WEALTHY

Protect Before You Grow

"He who is brave is free." — Seneca

The Two Neighbours

Let me tell you about two neighbours, Thato and Bongi, both staying in an apartment block in Midrand.

Thato lives in a nice house. Drives a new BMW. Wears designer clothes. Eats out three times a week. Takes holidays to Mauritius. Everyone thinks he's successful.

Bongi lives in a modest flat. Drives a 2008 Toyota Corolla with 200,000km on the clock. Wears ordinary clothes. Cooks at home. Takes one holiday every two years—to visit family in the Eastern Cape.

At first glance, Thato is winning.

But here's what you don't see.

Thato earns R50,000 a month. He spends R48,000 on rent, car payments, entertainment, and dining out. He saves R2,000 in a bank account.

If he loses his job, he has less than two months of expenses saved.

Bongi earns R25,000 a month. He lives modestly. He invests R5,000 a month into a Permanent Portfolio.

After ten years, Bongi has built substantial wealth.

Thato is rich in appearance.

Bongi is wealthy in reality.

Thato's BMW impresses people at the robot. Bongi's portfolio impresses no one at a braai—but it quietly buys his freedom.

Building wealth requires sacrificing appearances for substance.

It requires protecting what you build before trying to grow it faster.

The Difference Between Rich and Wealthy

There is a common confusion between being rich

and being wealthy.

Being rich usually means having a high income.

You earn a large salary. You drive a nice car. You live in a good neighbourhood. But if you stop working, the rich lifestyle collapses because the income stops. It's a rented lifestyle, not an owned one.

Being wealthy means having assets that produce income or grow in value without your active labour.

Wealthy people own things that work for them: shares, bonds, rental properties, businesses. Their lifestyle does not depend on a monthly payslip.

This book is not about helping you look rich.

We have enough people driving BMWs on hire-purchase to impress neighbours they don't even like.

This book is about helping you become wealthy.

Permanent Loss vs. Temporary Decline

Every investor faces two kinds of loss:

Temporary decline is when the value of your investment falls but eventually recovers. Equities and gold can crash and then climb to new highs. Bond prices dip and then stabilise. These declines are uncomfortable but not catastrophic if you stay invested.

Permanent loss is when you lose money that you never get back. Selling at the bottom of a crash. Investing in a pyramid scheme. Borrowing to speculate and getting wiped out.

These losses are devastating because they cannot be recovered from the same asset.

It's the difference between a cold that passes and losing your leg in a car accident.

One is temporary. The other is permanent.

The Permanent Portfolio is designed to avoid permanent loss.

It will experience temporary declines—every portfolio does. But because it is diversified across asset classes that respond differently to economic conditions, it has never suffered a permanent, catastrophic loss.

This protection allows you to stay invested. And staying invested is what allows you to benefit from long-term growth.

Why Liquidity Matters

Liquidity means how quickly you can turn an asset into cash without losing value.

Cash in a bank account is perfectly liquid. Shares on a stock exchange can be sold within a few days. Gold can be sold within a day. Bonds can be sold quickly as well.

But some assets are illiquid.

Property can take months to sell—especially when

the market is slow and the buyer's bond application is stuck at the bank. Private businesses are hard to value and hard to sell quickly. Collectibles like valuable art might take years to find a buyer.

Liquidity matters because life is unpredictable.

You might lose your job. A family member might need medical care. An emergency might require immediate cash.

If all your money is locked in illiquid assets, you may be forced to sell at a terrible price—like selling your generator for a fraction of its value because you need cash during a blackout.

The Permanent Portfolio includes 25% cash specifically to provide liquidity.

This cash buffer means you never have to sell your other assets during an emergency. You can handle surprises without disrupting your long-term investments.

You do not want to sell your investments when they have suffered temporary declines. Your 25% cash prevents this.

Safety Before Growth

Young investors often make the same mistake.

They want high returns. So they put all their money into the riskiest assets: individual stocks, cryptocurrencies, pyramid schemes. They ignore safety because they have decades to recover from losses.

But this approach backfires for two reasons.

First: A large loss early in your investing journey can set you back years. If you lose 50% of your portfolio at age 25, you need a 100% gain to recover. That gain might take five or ten years to achieve.

Second: Big losses cause emotional damage. They make you afraid to continue investing. They make you sell at the worst time. They destroy the discipline that building wealth requires.

Safety first does not mean avoiding growth.

It means ensuring that your portfolio can survive long enough to grow.

The Permanent Portfolio provides that safety while still delivering solid, inflation-beating returns over time.

Building on Solid Foundations

No building stands without a foundation.

No investment portfolio survives without a foundation of safety and discipline.

Your financial foundation includes:

- An emergency fund (covered in Chapter 12)
- A simple, diversified investment strategy (the Permanent Portfolio)

- The discipline to invest consistently
- The patience to let time work

If you try to build wealth on a weak foundation—chasing hot tips, borrowing to invest, skipping emergency savings—the whole structure will eventually collapse.

Usually at the worst possible time.

The Permanent Portfolio is your foundation.

Build it solid. Build it simple. Then build on top of it over time.

The First Rule of Investing: Survive

In investing, as in life, survival comes before success.

If you lose your entire portfolio, you cannot recover.

If you panic and sell at the bottom, you lock in losses that could have been recovered.

If you take risks that destroy your capital, you remove yourself from the game entirely.

The Permanent Portfolio prioritises survival.

It will not make you the richest person in your neighbourhood. But it will keep you in the game through every economic storm—and the game is where the wealth is built.

And staying in the game is how ordinary people become extraordinary investors.

Not through brilliant predictions.

Not through lucky bets.

But through steady, disciplined, and boring consistency.

Rich vs. Wealthy: A Quick Comparison

	Rich	Wealthy
Income	High salary	Assets produce income
Lifestyle	Expensive	Modest
If you lose your job	Lifestyle collapses	Lifestyle continues
What you own	Things that lose value	Things that gain value
How you're seen	Impressive to strangers	Unimpressive to strangers
Freedom	None—trapped by expenses	Options—work becomes optional

The South African Reality

In South Africa, we see this every day.

The person driving the new Mercedes might be drowning in debt.

The person driving the old Corolla might be quietly

building a portfolio that will fund their retirement at 50.

The person posting fancy restaurant meals on Instagram might be eating noodles at home the rest of the month.

The person who never posts anything might have a bank balance that would shock you.

Stop comparing your life to appearances.

Start comparing your life to your goals.

Key Takeaways

- Wealth (assets that work for you) is different from income (money you earn from labour)
- Avoid permanent loss by diversifying and not selling in panic
- Keep enough cash liquid to handle emergencies without disrupting your investments
- Safety first allows you to stay invested long enough to benefit from growth
- The first rule of investing is to survive so you can continue investing
- **Stay in the game**

Try This Today

1. Look at your spending from the last month
2. Ask yourself: "Am I spending money on things that look impressive or things that build wealth?"
3. Find ONE thing you can redirect from "looking rich" to "being wealthy"
4. Transfer that amount to your investment account

Did You Know?

The average South African spends more on car repayments than on retirement savings.

We are more interested in how we look to others than in how we will survive in the future.

This is the biggest mistake we make.

Reflection from the Stoics

Seneca wrote:

"It is not because things are difficult that we do not dare; it is because we do not dare that things are difficult."

Building a safety-first portfolio feels countercultural. Everyone around you is chasing the next big thing.

But true courage in investing is not taking the biggest risk.

It is having the discipline to build a portfolio that

can endure whatever comes.

Protecting your wealth is not cowardice.

It is the quiet confidence of someone who knows that the race is long and the only way to win is to finish.

What You've Learned So Far

Chapter	Key Lesson
Introduction	You don't need to be rich to start. The habit matters more than the amount.
Chapter 1	Working hard is not enough. You need assets that work while you sleep.
Chapter 2	Inflation is the invisible thief. It steals from savers every day.
Chapter 3	Time is your superpower. Start early and let compounding work for you.
Chapter 4	Looking rich is not the same as being wealthy. Protect before you

	grow.

What's Next

In Chapter 5, we'll meet the portfolio that survives everything.

You will learn:

- Why predicting the future is a trap
- The four seasons of the economy and which assets thrive in each
- Why diversification is the only free lunch in investing
- How the Permanent Portfolio was designed to work in any economic environment

The next chapter introduces you to a strategy that doesn't require you to be a genius—just disciplined.

CHAPTER 5: THE PORTFOLIO THAT SURVIVES EVERYTHING

Meet the Permanent Portfolio

"If one does not know to which port one is sailing, no wind is favourable." — Seneca

The Man Who Gave Up Predicting the Future

There was a man named Harry Browne.

He was a financial advisor, an author as well as an investor who had watched too many clever people lose money trying to predict the future.

He saw people bet their entire savings on stocks because they were convinced the economy would boom.

He saw people pile into gold because they were certain inflation was coming.

He saw brilliant economists make terrible decisions because they were absolutely sure about what would happen next.

And he saw most of them lose.

Not because they were stupid. Not because they didn't work hard. But because they were trying to do something fundamentally impossible:

Predict the future.

Harry Browne believed there had to be a better way. A way that didn't require predicting whether the economy would boom, bust, inflate, or stagnate. A way that could survive any economic season. A way simple enough for ordinary people to understand and maintain.

After years of research, he published what he called the Permanent Portfolio.

The name is important.

Permanent means designed for a lifetime. Not a trading strategy. Not a temporary bet. A permanent approach you can stick with through every economic season. Like a good pair of boots that carries you through mud, dust, and rain.

Harry Browne died in 2006. But his portfolio has lived on. Thousands of investors around the world have used it to build wealth steadily, without stress, without trying to time the market, and without losing sleep during crashes.

Now, South Africans can do the same.

Why Prediction Is a Trap

Turn on any news channel. Open any financial website.

Experts are everywhere, telling you exactly what will happen next.

"The stock market will crash."

"Inflation is coming."

"Gold is about to explode."

"Property is dead."

"Bitcoin is the future."

These predictions are almost always wrong.

If they were right, those experts would be on their private islands, not on SABC News or YouTube telling you what to do with your R500.

Not because the experts are stupid. But because the future is fundamentally unpredictable. Economies are complex systems with millions of moving parts and billions of decision-makers. A war breaks out. A virus spreads. A central banker changes their mind. A new technology disrupts an entire industry.

No model can capture all of this.

The most successful investors in history—Warren Buffett, Peter Lynch, John Bogle—did not succeed by predicting the future.

They succeeded by building systems that work regardless of what the future brings.

The Permanent Portfolio is built on this same humility.

It admits:

"I do not know what will happen next. Therefore, I will prepare for everything."

Prediction vs. Preparation

Prediction asks: "What will happen next?"

Preparation asks: "What could happen next, and how can I survive and thrive no matter what?"

This shift in thinking is profound.

It's the difference between a gambler and a farmer.

The gambler bets on the next card.

The farmer plants different crops because they don't know which weather will come.

When you try to predict, you put all your eggs in one basket. You bet on stocks because you think the economy will boom. Or you bet on gold because you think inflation is coming.

If you are right, you win big.

If you are wrong, you lose big.

When you prepare, you spread your eggs across multiple baskets. You accept that you cannot know which basket will perform best. So you own a bit of everything.

Some baskets will do well. Others will struggle. But overall, your portfolio grows steadily without dramatic crashes.

Preparation is boring. Preparation is humble. Preparation works.

In South Africa, we know that *umuntu ngumuntu ngabantu*—a person is a person through other people. Your portfolio is a portfolio through its parts, each supporting the others.

The Four Seasons of the Economy

Economies move through different phases. Harry Browne identified four broad economic environments, or "seasons."

Season 1: Prosperity

The economy is growing. Businesses expanding. Unemployment low. People spending.

Best asset: Equities (shares)

Companies earn higher profits. Share prices rise. Dividends increase. Everyone feels good.

Season 2: Inflation

Prices are rising rapidly. Cost of living increases. Money loses purchasing power. Your R100 buys less than it did last year.

Best asset: Gold

Hard assets hold their value when paper money weakens. Gold has been a store of value for thousands of years.

Season 3: Recession

Economy contracting. Businesses struggling. Unemployment rising. People cutting back.

Best asset: Cash

Many assets lose value. Cash becomes extremely valuable because its purchasing power increases. Cash is king.

Season 4: Deflation

Prices falling. This sounds good—cheaper things!—but deflation can be severe. Money becomes more valuable. Debts become harder to repay.

Best asset: Long-term government bonds

Central banks lower interest rates to stimulate the economy. Existing bonds with higher fixed coupon rates become very valuable as their purchasing power increases. Bond prices rise.

Each season requires a different asset to shine.

No single asset performs well in all four seasons—just like no single outfit works for a Durban summer, a Highveld thunderstorm, and a Cape winter.

The Permanent Portfolio owns assets that perform well in each season.

When the economy changes, your portfolio automatically benefits.

You do not need to predict the season.

You are prepared for all four seasons.

Why Diversification Is the Only Free Lunch

There's a famous saying in investing:

"Diversification is the only free lunch in investing."

This is true.

When you own different types of assets that behave differently, your overall portfolio becomes more stable. When stocks fall, bonds may rise. When inflation hurts cash, gold may protect you.

Diversification does not eliminate risk. But it reduces the kind of risk that destroys portfolios: the risk of being completely wrong.

It's like having both an umbrella and sunscreen in your bag—you're ready for whatever Cape Town weather decides to throw at you. (And Cape Town can give you all four seasons in one day.)

Many people misunderstand diversification. They

think owning ten different shares is diversified.

But ten shares are all still shares. They all tend to fall together during a crash.

True diversification means owning fundamentally different asset classes:

- Shares
- Bonds
- Cash
- Gold

The Permanent Portfolio takes this to its logical conclusion. It divides your money equally among four asset classes that respond differently to economic conditions.

The Elegance of Simplicity

You might expect a sophisticated investment strategy to be complicated.

The Permanent Portfolio is almost embarrassingly simple.

It's the kind of simplicity that makes people say:

"That's it? Surely I need to do more?"

No.

That's it.

Now go enjoy your life.

- **25% Equities (shares)** — Growth for prosperity

- **25% Long-term government bonds** — Protection for deflation
- **25% Cash** — Liquidity for recessions and emergencies
- **25% Gold** — Insurance against inflation and monetary crises

Four assets. Equal weights. Rebalance once per year. Ignore the noise.

This simplicity is a feature, not a bug.

Simple strategies are easy to stick with.

They don't require constant attention.

They leave no room for second-guessing.

They prevent you from making emotional decisions during market panics.

Why This Strategy Has Endured

The Permanent Portfolio has been tested through some of the most dramatic market events in modern history.

Event	What Happened	The Permanent Portfolio
1970s inflation crisis	Inflation reached double digits	Gold protected purchasing power
1987 stock market crash	Equities fell 20% in a day	Bonds provided a cushion

2000 dot-com bubble burst	Tech stocks crashed 80%	Diversification saved investors
2008 global financial crisis	Equities fell 40%	Bonds and gold hedged losses
2020 COVID-19 pandemic	Equities crashed 30%	Gold hedged losses and cash provided stability

Through all of these events, the Permanent Portfolio delivered positive returns over rolling 3-year periods.

It never suffered a catastrophic loss.

It never required investors to guess what came next.

It simply worked.

Does It Produce the Highest Returns Every Year?

No.

During a long bull market for stocks, a pure stock portfolio will outperform the Permanent Portfolio.

But that same stock portfolio will crash painfully during a recession.

The Permanent Portfolio trades some upside potential for significantly less downside risk.

For young investors building wealth over decades, avoiding devastating losses is more important than chasing maximum returns.

Because a 50% loss requires a 100% gain just to get back to even.

Avoiding the big loss is often the key to long-term success.

What Happens When You Don't Diversify

Let me tell you a story.

In the late 1990s, everyone was obsessed with technology stocks. People were quitting their jobs to day-trade from their bedrooms. They weren't investing. They were gambling.

And for a while, they were winning.

Then the dot-com bubble burst. Between 2000 and 2002, the Nasdaq index fell nearly 80%. Countless investors lost everything.

They had put all their eggs in one basket—the tech basket.

When that basket fell, they fell with it.

Now imagine someone who had been investing in a Permanent Portfolio during that same period. They would have owned tech stocks through their equity allocation, but they would also have owned bonds, cash, and gold.

When tech stocks crashed, their bonds and cash

would have provided a cushion.

They would have lost money—but they wouldn't have lost everything.

They would have stayed in the game.

And staying in the game is how you build wealth.

The Boring Secret to Wealth

Here's the thing about the Permanent Portfolio:

It's boring.

No one gets excited about it. No one posts about it on Instagram. You won't make a TikTok bragging about your 25% bond allocation.

And that's exactly the point.

Wealth is not built through excitement. It's built through consistency. It's built through discipline. It's built through doing the boring thing, month after month, year after year.

The people who got rich during the 2000s tech boom didn't keep their money. They lost it.

The people who got rich during the 1990s property boom didn't keep their money. They lost it.

The people who get rich from cryptocurrencies might not keep their money either. (History doesn't repeat, but it often rhymes.)

But the people who quietly invest in a diversified portfolio, rebalance once a year, and ignore the noise?

They keep their money.

They build wealth.

They win the long game.

Real South African Example

Let me show you how this might work in South Africa.

Imagine three friends in 2010. All three are 25 years old. All three earn the same salary. All three invest R500 a month.

Mlamuli puts all his money into South African equities (shares). He wants maximum growth.

Sibusiso puts all her money into a property. She buys a small flat in a growing area.

Sizwe builds a Permanent Portfolio—25% equities, 25% bonds, 25% cash, 25% gold.

From 2010 to 2025, what happens?

Year	Mlamuli (All Equities)	Sibusiso (Property)	Sizwe (Permanent Portfolio)
2010	Starts well	Buys flat	Starts well
2015	Has grown	Has grown	Has grown
2018	Market	Market	Portfolio

	drops 20%	uncertain	stable
2020	Pandemic crash 30%	Tenant issues	Portfolio stable
2025	Recovered and growing	Property worth more	Growing steadily

Mlamuli experienced wild ups and downs. Some years he felt like a genius. Other years he couldn't sleep.

Sibusiso had stability but also tenant headaches, maintenance costs, and a property that was hard to sell when she needed cash.

Sizwe built wealth quietly, consistently, and with much less stress.

Who do you think slept better at night?

The Psychology of Preparation

There is one more reason the Permanent Portfolio works.

It helps you sleep at night.

When you know you are prepared for any economic season, you stop worrying about which season will come.

You stop checking your portfolio every day.

You stop watching the news for clues about the future.

You stop panicking when markets crash.

You stop feeling FOMO when some asset goes crazy.

You simply invest, rebalance, and live your life.

That peace of mind is worth more than any extra return.

Common Myths About the Permanent Portfolio

Myth: "I don't need bonds. I'm young. I can take more risk."

Fact: Bonds protect you during deflations when equities crash. They are your safety net.

Myth: "Cash is a waste. I should invest everything."

Fact: Cash is insurance. It prevents you from selling investments during emergencies. It also lets you buy when markets crash.

Myth: "Gold is a barbarous relic. It doesn't earn anything."

Fact: Gold protects you during inflation and monetary crises when other assets fail. It's the umbrella for monetary storms.

Myth: "This portfolio is too conservative. I'll miss out on gains."

Fact: The Permanent Portfolio doesn't give you the highest returns in good years. But it protects you in bad years. And avoiding the big loss is how you win the long game.

Key Takeaways

- The Permanent Portfolio was created by **Harry Browne** to work in any economic environment without predicting the future
- Economies move through **four seasons**: prosperity, inflation, recession, and deflation
- Different assets perform well in each season
- The portfolio divides your money equally among equities, long-term government bonds, cash, and gold
- Simplicity and diversification protect you from catastrophic losses and emotional decision-making
- This strategy has survived decades of market crashes and economic upheavals
- The Permanent Portfolio is boring—and that's exactly why it works

Try This Today

1. Open a spreadsheet or get a piece of paper
2. Write down: "My Permanent Portfolio"
3. Underneath, write: 25% Equities, 25%

Bonds, 25% Cash, 25% Gold

4. Ask yourself: "What would I have to do to start investing in these four things?"
5. If your answer is "I need to open an investment account," go to the next chapter
6. **You are building the habit. Keep going.**

Did You Know?

A 50% loss requires a 100% gain just to get back to even. This is why avoiding big losses is more important than chasing big gains. The Permanent Portfolio is designed to avoid big losses so you can stay in the game and build wealth over time.

Reflection from the Stoics

The Stoics believed in accepting the limits of human knowledge.

Marcus Aurelius wrote: "Remember that you ought to behave in life as you would at a banquet. Something is passed around and comes to you: stretch out your hand and take a modest portion."

The Permanent Portfolio is that modest portion.

It does not greedily grab for the best-performing asset. It humbly accepts that the future is unknowable and takes a little of everything.

There is deep wisdom in this humility.

You are not a prophet.

You are a participant.

Prepare for all seasons, and you will not fear the weather.

What You've Learned So Far

Chapter	Key Lesson
Introduction	You don't need to be rich to start. The habit matters more than the amount.
Chapter 1	Working hard is not enough. You need assets that work while you sleep.
Chapter 2	Inflation is the invisible thief. It steals from savers every day.
Chapter 3	Time is your superpower. Start early and let compounding work for you.
Chapter 4	Looking rich is not the same as being wealthy. Protect before you grow.
Chapter 5	The Permanent Portfolio prepares for all economic seasons. You don't need to predict the future.

What's Next

In Chapter 6, we'll explore the first pillar of the Permanent Portfolio: Equities.

You will learn:

- What shares really represent—and why they make you an owner, not just a worker
- Why businesses create wealth over time
- Why equities perform during prosperity
- The big mistake most investors make with equities—and how to avoid it

The next chapter is about your money's running shoes—the asset that provides growth during good times.

CHAPTER 6: EQUITIES — YOUR MONEY'S RUNNING SHOES

Becoming an Owner, Not Just a Worker

"The impediment to action advances action. What stands in the way becomes the way." — Marcus Aurelius

Most people go through life as workers.

They sell their time and energy to an employer in exchange for a salary. There is nothing wrong with this. Most wealth starts with earned income.

But there is a ceiling to being only a worker.

No matter how hard you work, you only have twenty-four hours in a day. You can only sell your time once—and even the most dedicated employee can't bill a 25-hour day.

Ownership changes everything.

When you own shares in a company, you become a part-owner of that business. You are no longer just selling your time. You are sharing in the profits of thousands of employees who work for that company.

You benefit from their labour, their ideas, and their productivity.

This is the magic of equities.

They transform you from a worker into an owner.

What Shares Really Represent

A share is not a lottery ticket.

It is not a speculative instrument.

It is a small piece of a real business.

When you buy shares in Shoprite, you own a tiny fraction of every supermarket they operate—from the Shoprite in Sandton to the Usave in a rural town in KZN.

When you buy shares in MTN, you own a sliver of their mobile networks across Africa.

When you buy shares in Capitec, you own part of one of the most successful banks in the country.

These businesses employ people. They sell products. They earn profits.

As a shareholder, you are entitled to a portion of those profits.

Either through dividends (cash paid to shareholders) or through increased share prices as the business grows.

Equities are not abstract. They represent real economic activity—the same activity you see when you buy bread, airtime, or data.

Why Businesses Create Wealth

Over long periods of time, businesses tend to grow.

They find new customers. They develop new products. They become more efficient. They expand into new markets.

This growth translates into higher profits. And higher profits, over time, translate into higher share prices.

Since 1900, global equities have delivered average real returns (after inflation) of approximately 5-7% per year.

This means that money invested in a diversified portfolio of shares has roughly doubled in purchasing power every ten to fifteen years.

No other asset class has matched this long-term performance over the past 100 years.

The reason is simple: businesses are engines of innovation and productivity.

They take raw materials, labour, and ideas, and transform them into things that people value. This process creates real wealth.

The Power of Innovation and Productivity

Think about how much the world has changed in your lifetime.

When some of us were born:

- Smartphones did not exist
- Streaming was science fiction
- E-commerce was in its infancy

The companies that dominate today's economy —Tencent, Amazon, Google, Alibaba—were either startups or not yet founded.

Each of these innovations created enormous wealth for shareholders.

Not because of speculation. But because they solved real problems and created real value.

You cannot predict which company will invent the next breakthrough.

But you can bet that some companies will. By owning a broad range of shares through low-cost index funds or ETFs, you capture the growth of innovation without having to pick individual winners.

Why Equities Perform During Prosperity

Remember the four economic seasons from Chapter 3?

Equities are the prosperity asset.

When the economy grows, businesses earn more. When businesses earn more, share prices tend to rise. Dividends increase. Employment rises. A virtuous cycle develops.

During prosperity, equities often produce strong double-digit returns. These good years more than compensate for the bad years that come during recessions.

But equities do not perform well in every season.

During a deep recession, share prices can fall 30%, 40%, or even 50%.

This is normal. This is expected.

And this is why you do not put all your money in equities—just like you don't wear only running shoes.

The Big Mistake: Selling During Crashes

The biggest mistake investors make with equities is selling during crashes.

When share prices fall, fear spreads. News headlines scream about crisis. Friends and family panic. Your instinct will be to sell and "protect what is left."

Your brain will scream: **"Get out! At least save the furniture!"**

That instinct is almost always wrong.

Every major stock market crash in history has been followed by a recovery.

Event	Market Drop	Recovery Time
2008 financial crisis	-40%	2 years
2020 COVID-19 pandemic	-30%	1 year
2022 inflation fears	-25%	1.5 years

Investors who sold at the bottom locked in their losses. Those who stayed invested were rewarded.

Staying invested does not mean being foolish.

It means having a portfolio that allows you to weather the storm. The Permanent Portfolio's other assets—bonds, cash, and gold—provide stability when equities crash.

This gives you the emotional room to hold your shares and wait for the recovery.

A South African Example

The JSE (Johannesburg Stock Exchange) has been operating for over 130 years.

Over that period, it has survived:

- Two world wars
- Multiple global financial crises
- Apartheid
- The COVID-19 pandemic

Through all of it, the JSE has delivered positive returns over the long term.

Companies like Shoprite, MTN, Capitec, and Naspers have created enormous wealth for shareholders.

The South African economy has faced enormous challenges. But it has also produced incredible success stories.

The JSE is where South African wealth has been built for generations.

Keeping It Simple with Broad Diversification

You do not need to pick individual shares.

In fact, for most ordinary investors, picking individual shares is a mistake. It concentrates risk. It requires research skills that even professionals struggle with. It tempts you to trade frequently, which increases costs and taxes.

Instead, buy the whole market.

Exchange-traded funds (ETFs) allow you to own hundreds or thousands of shares in a single, low-cost product.

A South African equity ETF like the Satrix 40 gives you ownership in the largest and most important companies on the JSE.

With one purchase, you are diversified across retail, banking, mining, telecoms, technology, and more.

You capture the growth of the entire South African economy without having to predict which sector or stocks will win.

Lessons from Patient Investors

The world's most successful equity investors share one quality:

Patience.

Warren Buffett has been investing for more than seventy years. He did not get rich by trading frequently or timing the market. He bought solid businesses and held them for decades.

John Bogle, founder of Vanguard, spent his career preaching the power of low-cost index funds. He believed that trying to beat the market was a fool's errand. Owning the market and staying patient was the surest path to wealth.

You do not need to be a genius.

You do not need to be lucky.

You need to be disciplined and patient.

Equities are the running shoes of your portfolio. They provide the speed. But you have to keep them on for the long run—even when the road gets rough.

What R100 in Shoprite Would Have Grown To

Let me show you a real South African example.

In 2000, Shoprite shares cost around R5 each. By 2025, they had grown to over R300.

If you had invested R100 in Shoprite in 2000, it would have been worth more than R6,000 by 2025.

That's a 60x return.

But here's the thing:

You couldn't have known that Shoprite would grow like that. You couldn't have predicted it. You would have been betting on one company, not investing in the market.

If you had bought the whole market through an ETF, you would have captured Shoprite's growth without having to predict it.

That's the beauty of diversification.

Key Takeaways

- Equities make you an owner, not just a worker. You share in the profits of businesses
- Over long periods, equities have delivered the strongest inflation-beating returns of any major asset class
- Equities perform best during economic prosperity but can crash during recessions
- The biggest mistake is selling during crashes. Stay invested through diversification
- Buy the whole market through low-cost ETFs rather than picking individual shares
- Patience and discipline matter more than intelligence or luck

Try This Today

1. Open your investment account
2. Find a South African equity ETF (STX40, STXALL, or SYGALL)
3. Buy a small amount—even R25 counts
4. Now you own a piece of South Africa's largest companies
5. **You are officially an owner, not just a**

worker

Did You Know?

The JSE is the largest stock exchange in Africa and one of the oldest in the world.

It has been operating since 1887—longer than most stock exchanges in the world.

South African companies on the JSE have created enormous wealth for shareholders over more than a century.

Reflection from the Stoics

Marcus Aurelius wrote that our actions are hindered by obstacles, but those obstacles can become the path forward.

A market crash feels like an obstacle. But for the disciplined Permanent Portfolio investor, it is also an opportunity:

- To buy more equities cheaply through rebalancing
- To test your emotional resilience
- To prove to yourself that you can keep a promise made in calmer times

The obstacle of fear becomes the way to growth.

Your running shoes work best when you keep moving forward, even when the terrain gets rocky.

What You've Learned So Far

Chapter	Key Lesson
Introduction	You don't need to be rich to start. The habit matters more than the amount.
Chapter 1	Working hard is not enough. You need assets that work while you sleep.
Chapter 2	Inflation is the invisible thief. It steals from savers every day.
Chapter 3	Time is your superpower. Start early and let compounding work for you.
Chapter 4	Looking rich is not the same as being wealthy. Protect before you grow.
Chapter 5	The Permanent Portfolio prepares for all economic seasons. You don't need to predict the future.
Chapter 6	Equities are your running shoes. They provide growth during prosperity.

What's Next

In Chapter 7, we'll explore the second pillar of the

Permanent Portfolio: Bonds.

You will learn:

- What bonds really are—and why governments borrow money
- How bonds generate returns through interest and price changes
- Why bonds protect you during deflations and sometimes recessions.
- The emotional benefit of owning bonds when markets crash

The next chapter is about your portfolio's winter coat—the asset that keeps you warm when economic temperatures drop.

CHAPTER 7: BONDS — YOUR PORTFOLIO'S WINTER COAT

"It is a rough road that leads to the heights of greatness." — Seneca

What Bonds Really Are

Let me explain bonds in the simplest way possible.

When you buy a bond, you are lending money to someone. Usually the government or a large company.

In exchange for your loan, they promise to pay you interest at regular intervals and to return your original money on a specific future date.

Bonds are essentially IOUs with a contract.

You become the bank, and the government is your

customer that owes you.

Government bonds are considered very safe because governments rarely default on the debt in their own currency. A government can raise taxes or print money to pay its obligations.

South African government bonds are backed by the full faith and credit of the Republic. The risk of default is extremely low if bonds are issued in Rands.

Our government has many challenges, but paying its bondholders has historically not been one of them.

Why Governments Borrow

Governments borrow money for the same reason individuals do: they need money before they have it.

When South Africa builds a new road, a school, or a power station, the tax revenue to pay for it arrives over many years. Borrowing allows the government to build now and pay later—like using a bond to buy a house instead of saving the full purchase price in cash while living in a shack.

Bonds are how governments borrow.

They issue bonds to investors like pension funds, insurance companies, and ordinary people. Investors buy bonds because they want a safe, predictable return.

This system has worked for centuries. It is not new. It is not complicated. It is simply the way modern finance operates.

How Bonds Generate Returns

Bonds generate returns in two ways.

First, they pay interest. This is called a coupon.

A bond might pay 8% per year. If you buy R100,000 worth of that bond, you receive R8,000 in interest annually until the bond matures and you get your R100,000 back.

Second, bond prices change over time.

When interest rates fall, existing bonds that pay higher interest rates become more valuable. When interest rates rise, existing bonds become less valuable.

You can sell a bond before it matures for a profit or a loss.

For the Permanent Portfolio, we focus on long-term government bonds because they are most sensitive to changes in interest rates and economic conditions.

This sensitivity provides the protection we need during deflation—and, under the right conditions, can also help during recessions.

Why You Hold Bonds:

Deflation Protection

In the Permanent Portfolio, bonds are not there for recessions. **They are there for deflation.**

Deflation is a period when prices of goods and services fall, often the economy contracts, and the purchasing power of cash actually increases. In that environment, the fixed interest payments and the promise to repay par value become incredibly valuable. Long-term bonds soar.

During a recession, bonds *might* also do well, but only if the central bank cuts interest rates aggressively and inflation stays low. That's a secondary effect, not the core reason you hold them.

When central banks slash rates to stimulate a faltering economy, existing bonds with higher fixed coupons jump in price. This happened in 2008. But if a recession comes with high inflation (stagflation), bonds get hit. So you cannot rely on bonds to save you in every recession.

You hold bonds for the specific season of deflation, just as you hold cash for a recession. The portfolio is built so that each asset has a distinct job.

A South African Example — Bonds Helping in a Crisis

During the 2008 financial crisis, the JSE All Share Index fell almost 40%.

At the same time, South African government bonds produced 12% positive returns.

That wasn't deflation—it was a deep recession. Bonds soared because the South African Reserve Bank slashed interest rates from 12% to 7% in just a few months, and inflation was relatively contained. The rate cuts made older, higher-yielding bonds dramatically more valuable.

So even though bonds are your deflation shield, they also stepped up during that recession. But that was conditional. Had inflation spiked at the same time, the story would have been different.

A portfolio with both equities and bonds lost far less than a portfolio with only equities.

Imagine two investors:

	Investor A (100% Equities)	**Investor B (25% Equities, 25% Bonds, 25% Cash, 25% Gold)**
Equities	-40%	-40%
Bonds	0%	+12%
Overall	-40%	-14%

Investor B could sleep at night. Investor A was panicking.

Which investor do you think stayed in the game?

When Bonds Shine, When They Suffer

Remember the four seasons.

Bonds are the deflation asset.

When prices fall and the economy shrinks, central banks often lower interest rates toward zero, and long-term bonds are the best-performing asset in the portfolio. They provide stability and even strong growth while equities and gold struggle.

But bonds do poorly during inflation, especially rising inflation.

When prices rise rapidly, central banks raise interest rates. Rising interest rates cause bond prices to fall, sometimes sharply.

This is why you need other assets like gold to protect you during inflation, and cash to protect you during a recession.

The Permanent Portfolio holds bonds for the specific purpose of shielding you from deflation.

In other seasons, bonds may lag. But you hold them anyway because you cannot predict when deflation will arrive—and when it does, nothing else works as well.

The Emotional Benefit of Bonds

There is another benefit to bonds that is emotional rather than mathematical.

When the stock market crashes, fear spreads.

News headlines scream. Your friends are selling. The temptation to abandon your plan is overwhelming.

But if you own bonds, you experience the crash differently.

While your equities are down 30%, your bonds might be up 10%. Your overall portfolio is down only moderately.

You can look at your statement without panic.

You can hold steady while others sell.

This emotional stability is worth more than any mathematical advantage.

Because staying invested through the crash is what allows you to recover when markets rebound.

The Role of Bonds in the Permanent Portfolio

In the Permanent Portfolio, long-term government bonds receive a fixed 25% allocation.

Not corporate bonds. Not short-term bonds.

Long-term South African government bonds.

These bonds are held to maturity or rebalanced annually. You do not trade them. You do not try to predict interest rate movements.

You simply hold them as a permanent part of your portfolio.

Over decades, bonds have provided positive real returns while reducing portfolio volatility.

They are the winter coat that keeps you warm when economic temperatures drop—especially when deflation sends a bitter chill through other assets.

Understanding Bonds Without the Jargon

Many people avoid bonds because the terminology seems intimidating.

Term	What It Means
Coupon	The interest payment
Par value	The face value of the bond, the original loan amount
Maturity	The date when the bond repays your original loan amount
Yield	The effective return you earn based on the price you paid

You do not need to master any of this.

When you buy a government bond ETF, the fund manager handles all the complexity. You simply own a diversified basket of bonds that tracks the bond market.

The only thing you need to know:

Bonds are your primary defence against deflation,

and they can also cushion a recession if the central bank cuts rates while inflation stays low.

They are not exciting. They are not designed to make you rich quickly.

They are designed to keep you from going broke when the economic seasons turn bitter.

What Bonds Look Like in Practice

In South Africa, bonds have specific names like R2037, R2044, or R2053.

These names tell you when the bond matures or pays back the original loan amount.

- R2037 matures in 2037
- R2044 matures in 2044
- R2053 matures in 2053

The government issues new bonds and buys back old ones. You don't need to worry about any of this.

Buy a government bond ETF, and you own all of them at once.

Key Takeaways

- Bonds are loans to governments or companies. You earn interest and get your money back at maturity.
- Government bonds are very safe because governments rarely default.

- In the Permanent Portfolio, bonds are the **deflation** hedge. They perform best when prices are falling and central banks cut interest rates.
- Bonds *can* also benefit during recessions if interest rates are cut and inflation is low, but this is conditional—not guaranteed.
- When equities crash, bonds often rise, smoothing out your portfolio returns.
- In the Permanent Portfolio, long-term government bonds receive a 25% allocation.
- Bonds provide emotional stability during market panics, helping you stay invested.

Try This Today

1. In your investment account, find a South African government bond ETF.
2. Satrix Government Bond ETF (STXGOV) is a good start.
3. Buy a small amount—even R25 counts.
4. You now own a piece of South Africa's debt.
5. You are officially a lender to the South African government.

Did You Know?

South Africa has never defaulted on its government

bonds.

For over a century, the South African government has paid its bondholders. Even during the apartheid era. Even during the transition to democracy. Even during COVID-19.

The government has many problems. But not paying bondholders has never been one of them.

This is why government bonds are considered safe.

Reflection from the Stoics

Seneca wrote: "If you want to be loved, love."

If you want your portfolio to be stable, give it stability.

You do not put on a winter coat only when it snows; you have it ready.

Bonds are an act of love toward your future self—a quiet acknowledgment that the bitter cold of deflation will come, and you deserve protection when it does.

When others panic and sell, you will be the one who is warm.

That warmth is not just financial; it is emotional. It is the peace of knowing you prepared.

What You've Learned So Far

Chapter	Key Lesson
Introduction	You don't need to be rich to start. The habit matters more than the amount.
Chapter 1	Working hard is not enough. You need assets that work while you sleep.
Chapter 2	Inflation is the invisible thief. It steals from savers every day.
Chapter 3	Time is your superpower. Start early and let compounding work for you.
Chapter 4	Looking rich is not the same as being wealthy. Protect before you grow.
Chapter 5	The Permanent Portfolio prepares for all economic seasons. You don't need to predict the future.
Chapter 6	Equities are your running shoes. They provide growth during prosperity.
Chapter 7	Bonds are your winter coat. They protect you during recessions.

What's Next

In Chapter 8, we'll explore the third pillar of the

Permanent Portfolio: Cash.

You will learn:

- Why cash is not a waste—even though it hurts to hold it
- How cash saves you from forced selling during emergencies
- Why liquidity is freedom
- How cash turns emergencies into inconveniences

The next chapter is about your emergency backpack—the asset that protects you when life goes wrong.

CHAPTER 8: CASH – THE EMERGENCY BACKPACK

Why Cash Saves You (Even Though It Hurts)

"It is not the man who has too little, but the man who craves more, that is poor." — Seneca

The Day Everything Changed

Let me tell you about Sipho.

Sipho was 28 years old. He had a good job, a nice car, and a growing investment portfolio. He was doing everything right.

Then his company restructured. Sipho was re-trenched.

No warning. No gradual slowdown. Just: "Your position has been eliminated. Here's your retrenchment package. Good luck."

Sipho had been investing his money—all of it. Every Rand was in the stock market.

He also had a loan on his car and rent to pay.

When he lost his job, his portfolio was down 20% from the previous year. The market was in a slump.

He had two choices:

1. Sell his investments at a loss to pay his bills
2. Default on his payments and ruin his credit

Sipho sold at the bottom. He locked in losses that would have recovered. He watched the market rebound a year later—without him.

Sipho didn't fail because he didn't invest.

He failed because he didn't have cash.

Why Cash Is Not a Waste

Many investors believe cash is useless.

They say, "Cash is trash."

They think holding cash means missing out on growth. They want every Rand invested in assets that produce returns.

This is a mistake.

Cash is not an investment. Cash is insurance. Cash is flexibility. Cash is survival.

When you hold cash, you are not trying to beat inflation. You are accepting a small, predictable loss in purchasing power in exchange for safety and liquidity.

It's the same reason you pay for car insurance hoping you never need it.

You hold cash hoping you never need to spend it.

But when you need it, nothing else will do.

Try paying for a tow truck with your bond ETFs. Try paying for a burst geyser with your shares. Try paying for an emergency taxi to the hospital with your gold ETF.

Cash is what saves you when life goes wrong.

And life always goes wrong eventually.

Liquidity Is Freedom

Liquidity means how quickly you can turn an asset into cash without losing value.

Cash in a bank account is perfectly liquid. Shares on a stock exchange can be sold within seconds and cash received in a few days. Gold can be sold and cash received within a day. Bonds can be sold quickly as well.

But some assets are illiquid.

Property can take months to sell—especially when the market is slow and the buyer's bond application is stuck at the bank. Private businesses are hard to value and hard to sell quickly. Collectibles might take years to find a buyer.

Liquidity matters because life is unpredictable.

Imagine you lose your job tomorrow.

Your equities are down 20%. Your bonds are stable. Your gold is flat.

If you have no cash, you have two choices:

1. Sell your investments at a bad time
2. Borrow money at high interest

Both choices are painful. Both leave a mark.

Now imagine you have six months of expenses in cash.

You lose your job. You feel anxious, but not desperate. You can pay your rent, buy food, and cover transport while you search for new work.

You do not have to sell your equities at the bottom. You do not have to take a predatory loan from a mashonisa.

That is freedom. That is what cash buys you.

Preparing for Life's Surprises

Life is unpredictable.

Your car breaks down. Your laptop dies. A family member gets sick. Your landlord raises the rent. Your employer misses payroll. An opportunity arises that requires immediate cash.

These events are not rare. They are normal.

Every year, something unexpected happens.

If you have cash reserves, you handle these events with a shrug. Annoying, but manageable—like a two-hour blackout when you have a gas stove and a power bank.

If you have no cash, each event becomes a crisis. You scramble. You borrow. You sell investments at bad times. You accumulate high-interest debt.

Cash turns emergencies into inconveniences.

Emergencies, Opportunities, and Peace of Mind

Beyond emergencies, cash gives you the ability to seize opportunities.

When markets crash, prices become attractive. Equities go on sale.

But if all your money is already invested, you cannot buy more.

It's like arriving at a massive sale with an empty wallet.

If you hold cash, you can deploy it during downturns, buying assets when they are cheap.

This is called having "dry powder." It is one of the most powerful tools in an investor's toolkit.

The Permanent Portfolio's 25% cash allocation provides this dry powder automatically.

And beyond the mathematics, cash provides peace of mind.

When you know you can survive six months without income, you make better decisions.

You are not desperate.

You are not fearful.

You are in control.

Avoiding Forced Selling

The single greatest threat to a long-term investor is forced selling.

Forced selling happens when you need cash immediately and must sell assets regardless of their price.

You sell at the bottom. You convert temporary declines into permanent losses. You miss the recovery.

It's the financial equivalent of selling your generator for scrap because you need petrol money during a blackout.

Cash eliminates forced selling.

Because you have reserves, you never have to sell investments during an emergency. You let your investments recover on their own time while you live off your cash.

This is why the Permanent Portfolio holds 25% cash.

Not because cash earns high returns.

But because cash protects you from the worst mistake an investor can make: selling at the worst possible time.

Cash as Emotional Protection

Markets do not just test your wallet.

They test your nerves.

When the JSE falls 30% in three months, every instinct screams at you to sell. The fear is real. The anxiety is physical.

But if you have cash, you are less afraid.

You know you can survive without touching your equities. You know you might even buy more if prices fall further.

That knowledge calms your nerves. It allows you to think clearly when others are panicking.

Cash is emotional protection as much as financial protection.

It keeps you from making the terrible decisions that fear produces.

The Role of Cash in the Permanent Portfolio

In the Permanent Portfolio, cash is not a small afterthought.

It is a full 25% allocation.

This cash is not under your mattress. It is held in liquid, low-risk instruments: money market funds, treasury bills, and/or bank accounts that allow immediate withdrawal.

The goal is safety and accessibility, not return.

Over time, this cash allocation will slightly drag your overall returns. That is the price of insurance.

It is a small price to pay for:

- The ability to survive emergencies
- The ability to seize opportunities
- The ability to sleep peacefully at night
- The ability to avoid forced selling

Cash is the price of your independence.

How Much Cash Do You Need?

The Permanent Portfolio says 25% of your total investments should be in cash.

But before you invest anything, you need an emergency fund.

Your first target: **R5,000** in a separate savings account.

This will cover most small emergencies: a car repair, a doctor's visit, a broken phone.

Once you reach R5,000, your next target: **three months of essential expenses.**

This will take longer. Build it gradually.

But here's the important part:

While building your emergency fund, you can still invest small amounts. Even R100 per month while you save is better than nothing.

Emergency Fund Target	How Much You Need	What It Covers
Level 1	R5,000	Small emergencies: car repair, doctor's visit, broken phone
Level 2	3 months of expenses	Short-term unemployment, unexpected bills
Level 3	6 months of expenses	Job loss, serious illness, major life change

What Cash Looks Like in Practice

In the Permanent Portfolio, cash can be held in different ways.

Option 1: Money Market Fund

A money market fund invests in short-term, low-risk debt. It pays interest slightly higher than a savings account. It's safe and liquid.

Option 2: Savings Account

Banks like GoTyme, Capitec, and others offer savings accounts with competitive interest rates. No fees. Immediate access. The savings accounts are also protected by deposit insurance in case your bank goes bankrupt.

Option 3: Treasury Bills

These are short-term government loans. Very safe. But harder to access for small amounts.

Option 4: Satrix Money Market ETF (STXMMF)

This is an ETF that holds money market instruments. You can buy it through EasyEquities just like any other ETF.

Recommendation for young investors:

Use a high-interest savings account with no fees. It's simple. It's safe. It gives you immediate access.

What Happens When You Don't Have Cash

Let me tell you another story.

Nomsa was a young professional in Johannesburg. She had a good job, a nice apartment, and a growing portfolio.

She also had no emergency fund. Every Rand went into investments.

Then her car broke down. R8,000 to fix it.

She had two choices:

1. Put it on her credit card at 24% interest
2. Sell some of her investments

She sold her investments. They were down 10% at the time.

She locked in a loss. Then the market recovered. She missed out.

The car repair cost her R8,000 in cash.

The forced sale cost her thousands more in lost growth.

A Better Way

Now imagine Nomsa had R8,000 in cash.

Her car breaks down. She pays R8,000.

She feels annoyed. But not desperate. She doesn't sell her investments. She doesn't go into credit card debt.

She slowly rebuilds her emergency fund.

Her portfolio keeps growing.

Her peace of mind stays intact.

That's the difference cash makes.

Common Mistakes with Cash

Mistake 1: Holding too little cash

"Cash is trash. I want everything invested."

This is how you end up selling at the bottom.

Mistake 2: Holding too much cash

"You never know what might happen. I'll just keep it all in cash."

This is how inflation steals your wealth.

Mistake 3: Using the wrong cash vehicle

"I'll keep my emergency fund in my cheque account."

This is where inflation eats your money even faster.

Mistake 4: Not keeping cash separate

"If I see the money, I'll spend it."

This is why your emergency fund should be in a separate account.

The Perfect Balance

The Permanent Portfolio gives you the perfect balance.

25% cash for emergencies, opportunities, and peace of mind.

Not too little. Not too much. Just right.

25% cash is the sweet spot between safety and growth.

This cash allocation is what makes the portfolio permanent.

It's what allows you to hold through crashes.

It's what allows you to buy when others are selling.

It's what allows you to sleep at night.

Common Myths About Cash

Myth: "Cash doesn't earn anything. I should invest everything."

Fact: Cash is insurance. You don't expect insurance to earn you money. You expect it to protect you.

Myth: "I can use my credit card for emergencies."

Fact: Credit cards charge 20%+ interest. That's not an emergency fund. That's an emergency accelerator.

Myth: "I can sell my investments if I need cash."

Fact: You might need cash when investments are down. That's forced selling. That's how you lose money.

Myth: "I'll build my emergency fund later."

Fact: Emergencies don't wait for "later." Build it now. Start with R100.

Key Takeaways

- Cash is insurance and flexibility, not an investment. It provides safety and liquidity.
- A cash emergency fund prevents forced selling during market downturns or personal emergencies

- Cash turns emergencies into inconveniences and gives you the ability to seize opportunities
- The Permanent Portfolio allocates 25% to cash to provide this protection
- Cash also provides emotional stability, helping you avoid panic-driven decisions
- Build an emergency fund of R5,000 first, then three months of expenses
- Keep your cash in a high-interest savings account with no fees

Try This Today

1. Open your banking app or a spreadsheet
2. Calculate your essential monthly expenses: rent, transport, food, electricity, data
3. Multiply by 6. That's your emergency fund target
4. Look at your current savings balance
5. Calculate the gap: Target — Current = How much you need to save
6. Set up a separate savings account for your emergency fund
7. Automate a monthly transfer—even R100 counts

This is not optional. This is survival.

This is the most important thing you can do for your financial health.

Because without cash, you are one emergency away from disaster.

Did You Know?

Most South Africans cannot afford a R5,000 emergency.

If their car breaks down or their phone dies, they have to borrow money.

They go into debt. They pay interest. They lose money.

You don't have to be most South Africans.

Build your emergency fund. Be the exception.

Reflection from the Stoics

Epictetus taught that freedom is the only worthy goal, and freedom is achieved by mastering what is within our control.

Cash is the most direct financial expression of that freedom.

It doesn't make you rich. But it ensures you are never forced.

When you have cash, you can:

- Say no to a bad job offer
- Walk away from a predatory lender

- Sleep through a market crash
- Help a family member in need
- Wait for the right opportunity

That is not a waste of money.

That is the purchase of autonomy.

What You've Learned So Far

Chapter	**Key Lesson**
Introduction	You don't need to be rich to start. The habit matters more than the amount.
Chapter 1	Working hard is not enough. You need assets that work while you sleep.
Chapter 2	Inflation is the invisible thief. It steals from savers every day.
Chapter 3	Time is your superpower. Start early and let compounding work for you.
Chapter 4	Looking rich is not the same as being wealthy. Protect before you grow.
Chapter 5	The Permanent Portfolio prepares for all economic seasons. You don't need to predict the future.

Chapter 6	Equities are your running shoes. They provide growth during prosperity.
Chapter 7	Bonds are your winter coat. They protect you during recessions.
Chapter 8	Cash is your emergency backpack. It protects you when life goes wrong.

What's Next

In Chapter 9, we'll explore the fourth pillar of the Permanent Portfolio: Gold.

You will learn:

- Why gold has endured for thousands of years as a store of value
- How gold protects you during inflation and monetary crises
- Why gold is insurance, not speculation
- The South African gold connection—and why it matters for you

The next chapter is about your umbrella for monetary storms—the asset that protects you when confidence in paper money collapses.

CHAPTER 9: GOLD – THE CURRENCY THAT NEVER DIES

Gold: The Umbrella for Monetary Storms

"Dig within. Within is the wellspring of good; and it is always ready to bubble up, if you just dig." — Marcus Aurelius

The Zimbabwe Story

Let me tell you about Mrs. Zitha.

She was a teacher in Zimbabwe. She worked for forty years. She saved diligently. She had a retirement fund.

Then the Zimbabwean dollar collapsed.

Overnight, her life savings became worthless. Banknotes became wallpaper. A wheelbarrow full of cash could barely buy a loaf of bread.

Mrs. Zitha lost everything.

Her neighbour, Mr. Moyo, had a different story.

He wasn't rich. He didn't have a fancy job. But he had bought a few gold coins over the years. Not many. Just a few.

When the currency collapsed, his gold coins could still buy food. Still pay rent. Still send his children to school.

Mr. Moyo survived.

Mrs. Zitha didn't.

This is not a happy story. It is a warning.

Humanity's Oldest Store of Value

Gold has been used as money for more than five thousand years.

Ancient Egyptians buried gold with their pharaohs. Romans used gold coins to pay their legions. Kings and queens measured their wealth in gold.

Even today, central banks hold gold as a reserve asset.

The South African Reserve Bank (SARB) holds about 4 million troy ounces of gold.

That's over R250 billion at current Rand gold

prices. Over 20% of its reserves.

Money the government itself cannot print.

Why has gold endured?

Because gold cannot be printed.

Governments cannot create more gold the way they create paper money. No matter how many zeroes they add, they can't print a gold bar.

Ask your favourite AI tool about what gold truly is, its characteristics, where it is used and why it is unique.

Gold is scarce, durable, divisible, and universally recognised. Gold is beautiful.

Paper currencies come and go.

- The South African Rand is continuously being depreciated
- The Zimbabwean Dollar collapsed entirely
- The Venezuelan Bolívar became worthless
- The Argentinian Peso has lost value repeatedly
- The Lebanese Pound collapsed by over 95% recently.
- The Turkish Lira lost value aggressively through decades
- The Hungarian Pengő suffered history's worst hyperinflation
- The German Papiermark collapsed during

the Weimar Republic
- The Yugoslav Dinar experienced severe hyperinflation in 1994

But gold remains gold.

Why Gold Has Endured for Thousands of Years

Every government in history has eventually debased its currency.

They print more money to fund their ever-growing expenses and pay debts. Each new Rand printed reduces the value of every existing Rand note.

Gold resists this debasement.

It cannot be printed. It can only be mined, slowly and expensively. The supply of gold grows at roughly 1-2% per year, far slower than the supply of paper money.

This scarcity gives gold its value.

When confidence in paper money falls, confidence in gold rises.

Gold is the hedge against monetary mismanagement.

And if history teaches us anything, governments mismanage money rather frequently.

Gold During Inflation

Remember inflation from Chapter 2?

When prices rise rapidly, paper money loses purchasing power.

Gold tends to do the opposite.

Period	What Happened	What Gold Did
1970s	US inflation reached double digits	Gold rose from \$35 to \$850 per ounce
2008-2011	Central banks printed enormous amounts of money	Gold rose from \$700 to \$1,900 per ounce
2020	COVID-19 stimulus	Gold reached new highs

Gold protected investors who had the foresight to own it.

Gold is not a perfect inflation hedge.

It can be volatile. It can underperform for years—during which everyone will tell you it's a barbarous relic.

But over long periods, gold has preserved purchasing power against the erosion of paper currencies.

Protection During Monetary Uncertainty

Inflation is not the only threat to paper money.

Currency crises, banking collapses, capital controls, and sovereign debt defaults all threaten the value of money held in banks or bonds.

During these events, gold often performs well because **it is nobody's liability.**

Scenario	What Happens to Paper Money	What Happens to Gold
Bank fails	Your deposits may be frozen	Gold is safe
Government defaults	Your bonds may be worthless	Gold is safe
Capital controls	You can't move money out	Gold is portable
Currency crisis	Your money loses value	Gold holds value

Gold is physical. Gold is portable. Gold is accepted anywhere in the world.

It is the ultimate emergency asset.

The financial equivalent of a passport that never expires.

Insurance, Not Speculation

The most important thing to understand about gold is that **you hold it as insurance, not as a speculation.**

You do not buy gold because you expect it to make you rich.

You buy gold because you want protection against the worst-case scenarios that might destroy the value of your other assets.

You hope you never need that insurance.

You hope inflation stays low.

You hope the Rand remains stable.

You hope banks and governments behave responsibly.

But hope is not a strategy.

And hope never stopped a currency crisis.

Gold is the umbrella you carry even when the sun is shining.

Because you know that monetary storms sometimes arrive without warning—especially in our part of the world.

Zimbabweans who held gold when the Zimbabwean Dollar collapsed were better protected than those without gold.

The same is true for Venezuelans and Argentinians when their currencies also collapsed.

Why Gold Belongs in the Portfolio

Some investors dismiss gold as a barbarous relic.

They point out that gold pays no interest or

dividends. They argue that productive assets like shares and bonds are superior.

They are not wrong about the facts.

But they miss the point.

The Permanent Portfolio is not designed to maximise returns. It is designed to survive all economic conditions.

Gold plays a unique role that no other asset can fill.

Asset	Protects Against
Equities	Prosperity
Bonds	Deflation, Recession
Cash	Recession, Emergencies, deflation
Gold	Inflation, monetary crisis, currency collapse, socio-political crisis

When confidence in paper assets collapses, only gold retains its value.

When the financial system sneezes, gold catches a cold but never pneumonia.

By including gold, you ensure that your portfolio has protection against the worst monetary storms.

It is the price of admission for a portfolio that can truly survive anything.

The South African Gold Connection

South Africa has a special relationship with gold.

We are one of the world's largest gold producers. The Witwatersrand basin has produced more gold than any other mining region in history.

South African gold coins—Krugerrands—are recognised around the world as trusted gold bullion.

Gold is part of our national story.

When you own gold in South Africa, you are not just protecting yourself from inflation. You are connecting with a tradition that has protected wealth for generations.

Gold mining built Johannesburg. Gold reserves back the Rand. Gold protects your wealth.

It's as South African as braai and ingudu.

Staying Disciplined When Gold Is Unpopular

Gold goes through long periods of underperformance.

In the 1980s and 1990s, gold prices fell for nearly twenty years. Investors who bought gold at the peak in 1980 and sold in 1999 lost more than 70% of their money in real terms.

During that period, gold seemed like a terrible investment.

Every braai conversation mocked the gold bugs.

But disciplined Permanent Portfolio investors held their 25% allocation.

They rebalanced each year, selling equities and bonds to buy more gold as its price fell.

They bought low without knowing when gold would recover.

Then from 2000 to 2011, gold rose from $250 to $1,900 per ounce.

Those who stayed disciplined were rewarded.

Those who abandoned gold because it was unpopular missed the recovery.

This pattern will repeat. There will be years when gold is hated. There will be years when gold is loved.

You cannot predict when the turn will come.

You can only hold your allocation and rebalance according to your plan.

What Gold Looks Like in Practice

In the Permanent Portfolio, gold can be held in different ways.

Option 1: Physical Gold

Krugerrands, gold bars, or gold jewellery. Physical gold is tangible. You can hold it in your hand.

But physical gold comes with storage and security costs with professional storage. You need a safe and you need to add it to your household insurance policy if you keep it at home.

Option 2: Gold ETFs

These are exchange-traded funds that hold physical gold on your behalf.

Examples:

- 1Invest Gold ETF (GLD)
- Absa NewGold ETF (GOLD)

These ETFs are backed by physical gold stored in South Africa. You own the gold without having to store it yourself.

Option 3: Gold Mining Shares

These are shares in companies that mine gold. But they are not the same as gold.

Gold mining shares can go down when gold goes up. They are affected by many other factors.

Recommendation for young investors:

Use a gold ETF. It's simple. It's secure. It's backed by physical gold. But as your overall portfolio increases, begin diversifying your gold position by adding Krugerrands. You can buy Krugerrands through the FNB app. FNB can store your Krugerrands at a fee or have them delivered to you. If stored with FNB, it is as liquid as cash as when you sell your Krugerrands, you get your cash immediately, not at the end of the end or after 3 days, immediately. I recommend this option together with physical holding of Krugerrands.

A Quick Note on Bitcoin

Some people ask: "Isn't Bitcoin the new gold?"

I understand the question. Bitcoin is scarce. It's digital. It's decentralised.

But Bitcoin is not gold.

- Bitcoin has only existed for a decade. Gold has existed for 5,000 years.
- Bitcoin is digital. Gold is physical.
- Bitcoin has huge price swings. Gold is relatively stable.
- Bitcoin can be hacked. Gold cannot.
- Bitcoin regulations change. Gold has been recognised as money for millennia.
- Gold is a commodity that is used to create other goods, like gold rings. Bitcoin is not.

Bitcoin is speculation. Gold is insurance.

The Permanent Portfolio holds insurance. Not speculation.

The Emotional Aspect of Gold

There is something psychological about gold.

Holding gold makes you feel safer.

It's not logical. It's emotional. But emotions matter

in investing.

When you hold gold, you know that no government can print it away. No bank can freeze it. No financial crisis can make it worthless.

That knowledge changes how you feel.

And how you feel changes how you invest.

Common Myths About Gold

Myth: "Gold doesn't earn anything. It's just a metal."

Fact: Gold doesn't earn interest, but it protects against inflation and monetary crises. You don't buy insurance because it earns interest. You buy it because it protects you.

Myth: "Gold has no value in a modern economy."

Fact: Every major central bank holds gold as a reserve asset. They don't hold Bitcoin. They don't hold shares. They hold gold. Gold is used in cellphones and other electronics.

Myth: "I can't afford gold."

Fact: Gold ETFs allow you to buy gold with R25. You don't need to buy a Krugerrand. Start small.

Myth: "Gold is just speculation."

Fact: Gold is insurance. Speculation is trying to get rich quickly. Insurance is preparing for the worst. They are opposite things.

Key Takeaways

- Gold has been a store of value for thousands of years because it cannot be printed or debased, and is universally accepted for its outstanding physical properties.
- Gold protects against inflation, monetary crises, and socio-political crises when paper money loses value.
- Gold is insurance, not a speculation. You hold it for protection, not to get rich.
- In the Permanent Portfolio, gold receives a 25% allocation alongside equities, bonds, and cash.
- Gold can underperform for long periods, which is why discipline is essential.
- Rebalancing ensures you buy gold when it is cheap and sell when it becomes expensive.

Try This Today

1. In your investment account, find a gold ETF
2. 1Invest Gold ETF (GLD) or Absa NewGold ETF (GOLD) are good options
3. Buy a small amount—even R25 counts
4. You now own physical gold, stored securely

in South Africa

5. **You are officially protected against monetary storms**

Did You Know?

The South African Reserve Bank holds more than 4 million troy ounces of gold.

That's over R250 billion at current prices.

Our central bank knows gold is real money.

Reflection

Marcus Aurelius reminded himself that everything we see will decay and be forgotten.

Paper money certainly will.

Gold endures. It has survived every attempt to replace it.

There is a Stoic lesson here:

Build your wealth on things that last.

Not on passing fads. Not on the promises of politicians. Not on the latest financial innovation.

The Permanent Portfolio asks you to own gold not because you love it, but because you accept reality:

The world is uncertain, and the humble yellow metal has seen it all before.

What You've Learned So Far

Chapter	Key Lesson
Introduction	You don't need to be rich to start. The habit matters more than the amount.
Chapter 1	Working hard is not enough. You need assets that work while you sleep.
Chapter 2	Inflation is the invisible thief. It steals from savers every day.
Chapter 3	Time is your superpower. Start early and let compounding work for you.
Chapter 4	Looking rich is not the same as being wealthy. Protect before you grow.
Chapter 5	The Permanent Portfolio prepares for all economic seasons. You don't need to predict the future.
Chapter 6	Equities are your running shoes. They

	provide growth during prosperity.
Chapter 7	Bonds are your winter coat. They protect you during recessions.
Chapter 8	Cash is your emergency backpack. It protects you when life goes wrong.
Chapter 9	Gold is your umbrella. It protects you during monetary storms.

What's Next

In Chapter 10, we'll put it all together.

You will learn:

- How to build your South African Permanent Portfolio step by step
- Which ETFs to buy and where to buy them
- How to rebalance once per year
- How to use Tax-Free Savings Accounts to maximise your wealth

The next chapter is the practical guide—everything you need to know to start building your portfolio today.

CHAPTER 10: BUILDING YOUR SOUTH AFRICAN PERMANENT PORTFOLIO

Putting It All Together

"First say to yourself what you would be; then do what you have to do." — Epictetus

The Day You Become an Investor

Remember Thabo and Lerato from Chapter 1?

Thabo kept waiting. Lerato started immediately.

Today is the day you become Lerato.

Not next week. Not next month. Not when you have more money.

Today.

By the end of this chapter, you will know exactly how to build your Permanent Portfolio.

You will have a plan.

You will have a checklist.

You will be ready to act.

The 25-25-25-25 Approach

By now, you understand the four pillars:

Asset	Purpose	What It Does
25% Equities (shares)	Growth	Runs during prosperity
25% Long-term government bonds	Protection	Shields you during deflation
25% Cash	Survival	Saves you in emergencies and recessions
25% Gold	Insurance	Protects you during monetary storms (inflation)

Equal weights. Simple.

No need to predict which asset will perform best.

No more difficult than dividing a pizza among four hungry friends.

Your job is not to guess. Your job is to allocate, **contribute monthly**, and rebalance once per year, perhaps on your birthday.

That's it.

Why This Works in South Africa

The Permanent Portfolio was originally designed in America by Harry Browne.

But it works the same way in South Africa.

South Africans can build the South African Permanent Portfolio using South African assets.

We have:

- A stock exchange (JSE) with excellent companies
- Government bonds that are safe and accessible
- Money market funds and savings accounts
- Gold ETFs backed by physical gold
- Krugerrands that are easily accessible

Everything you need exists right here.

You don't need to open an offshore account. You don't need to deal with foreign currencies. You don't need to be a millionaire.

This is South African wealth building for South Africans.

What You Need to Know About ETFs

An ETF is an exchange-traded fund.

Think of it as a basket of investments.

When you buy one unit of an ETF, you own a small piece of a large basket of assets.

For example:

The Satrix 40 ETF holds shares in the 40 largest companies on the JSE.

Buying one unit of Satrix 40 gives you ownership in all 40 companies at once.

Diversification in a single transaction.

Like buying a mixed grill instead of ordering each piece of meat separately.

ETFs are ideal for ordinary investors because they provide:

- Instant diversification
- Low costs
- Easy access
- Fractional shares (you can buy with R25)

ETFs are the secret weapon of the R100 investor.

Your South African Permanent Portfolio

Here are the specific investments you need.

1. Equities (25%)

Recommended ETF	JSE Code	What It Tracks	Cost (approx.)
Satrix 40	STX40	40 largest JSE companies	0.30%
Satrix All Share	STXALL	Entire JSE	0.40%
Sygnia All Share	SYGALL	Entire JSE	0.15%

Recommendation for most people: Start with STX40. It's simple, liquid, and low-cost.

2. Long-term Government Bonds (25%)

Recommended ETF	JSE Code	What It Tracks	Cost (approx.)
Satrix Government Bond	STXGOV	SA government bonds (10+ years)	0.30%
CoreShares GOVI	GOVI	SA government bond index	0.25%

Recommendation for most people: Start with STX-

GOV. It's simple and gives you exposure to long-term government bonds.

3. Cash (25%)

Recommended Vehicle	What It Is	Notes
Money market fund	Short-term, low-risk debt	Slightly higher interest
High-interest savings account	Bank savings account	No fees, immediate access
Satrix Money Market ETF	STXMMF	ETF version

Recommendation for most people: Use a high-interest savings account with no fees. GoTyme, African Bank, or similar. It's simple and accessible.

4. Gold (25%)

Recommended ETF	JSE Code	What It Tracks	Cost (approx.)
1Invest Gold ETF	GLD	Physical gold in South Africa	0.40%
Absa NewGold ETF	GOLD	Physical gold	0.40%

Recommendation for most people: Start with GLD. It's backed by physical gold stored in South Africa.

Your First R100: How to Buy It

Let's say you have R100.

Here's exactly what to do:

Asset	Amount	What to Buy
Equities	R25	STX40
Bonds	R25	STXGOV
Cash	R25	Capitec or GoTyme savings account
Gold	R25	GLD

That's it.

You now own four different assets that respond to four different economic seasons.

You are prepared for everything.

Where to Buy

EasyEquities

This is the most popular platform for new investors.

- Fractional shares allow you to invest any amount, even R100.
- Low fees

- User-friendly mobile app
- Supports all the ETFs in this book

How to open an account:

1. Go to easyequities.co.za
2. Click "Sign Up"
3. Enter your details (ID, proof of residence, phone number)
4. Complete FICA verification
5. Fund your account (EFT or instant deposit)
6. Start buying

It takes less than 15 minutes.

Rebalancing: The Secret Sauce

Rebalancing is the secret sauce of the Permanent Portfolio.

Over time, your assets will grow at different rates.

Suppose equities do very well for a few years. Your portfolio might become:

Asset	Original	After Strong Growth
Equities	25%	40%
Bonds	25%	20%
Cash	25%	20%
Gold	25%	20%

You are now overweight equities and underweight everything else.

Once per year, you rebalance.

You sell some of the assets that grew too much and buy more of the assets that lagged.

You bring your portfolio back to 25% each.

Why rebalance?

Because rebalancing forces you to sell high and buy low.

You sell assets that have become expensive and buy assets that have become cheap.

This discipline improves returns over time while controlling risk.

Rebalancing Without Selling

You don't always have to sell to rebalance.

You can use your monthly contributions.

If equities have drifted down to 20% because of underperformance, while gold is at 30%, cash and bonds are at 25%:

New contributions go to equities and not gold.

This brings the portfolio back into balance without selling anything.

This strategy minimises tax and transaction costs.

A Word on Taxes

South Africa has specific tax rules for investors.

First: You are generally not taxed on capital gains until you sell an asset. This means you can hold investments for years without paying tax on the growth.

Second: You pay dividend withholding tax (20%) on any dividends received from shares or ETFs. This is deducted automatically.

Third: Interest earned from bonds and cash may be subject to income tax if it exceeds certain thresholds.

For most young investors with smaller portfolios, these taxes are manageable.

The Tax-Free Savings Account (TFSA)

A TFSA is your best friend.

It allows you to invest up to R46,000 per year (lifetime limit R500,000) with no tax on growth, dividends, or interest.

You can hold many of the Permanent Portfolio ETFs inside a TFSA.

This is an excellent option for young investors. If fact, you should start by investing through a TFSA until you invest R46,000 limit. Most people will not reach the R46,000 limit, which means they can invest tax-free.

It's like a government-sponsored wealth-building booster.

Retirement vs. Discretionary Investing

You should invest in two ways.

First: Contribute to retirement vehicles like the employer-sponsored pension fund or retirement annuity, for long-term growth. These accounts offer tax benefits.

Second: Maintain a discretionary (non-retirement) Permanent Portfolio for medium-term and long-term goals as well as emergencies.

Do not put all your money into retirement accounts where it is locked until age 55.

Life happens. You need accessible wealth too.

A retirement fund won't pay for your car breakdown at age 30.

What to Do When Markets Move

Markets will move dramatically.

They always have. They always will.

What Happens	What You Should Do
Equities crash	Nothing except rebalance

Gold soars	Nothing except rebalance
Bonds lag	Nothing except rebalance
Everyone panicking	Nothing except rebalance
Everyone celebrating	Nothing except rebalance

Do nothing except rebalance once per year.

Do not try to predict which asset will do well next.

Do not increase your equity allocation because you are feeling optimistic.

Do not sell your gold because it has been flat for years.

Your plan is simple. Stick to it.

The plan is the boss. You are just the executor.

Common Mistakes to Avoid

Mistake	Why It's Dangerous
Owning too little gold	Leaves you exposed to inflation and socio-political risks
Using corporate bonds instead of	Companies can go bankrupt; govern-

government bonds	ments can print money
Holding cash in low-interest accounts	Your cash should earn some interest
Rebalancing too often	Once per year is enough. More increases costs and taxes
Trying to time the market	You can't predict when to buy or sell
Checking your portfolio daily	Creates anxiety and tempts you to make poor decisions
Abandoning the plan	The plan only works if you stick to it

A Real Example: Nonhlanhla's First Year

Let's follow Nonhlanhla.

Nonhlanhla is 25. She earns R15,000 a month. She decides to invest R500 a month.

Month 1:

She opens an EasyEquities account. She deposits R500. She buys:

- R125 of STX40 (equities)
- R125 of STXGOV (bonds)
- R125 of GLD (gold)
- R125 in her GoTyme savings account

(cash)

Months 2-11:

She repeats this every month. Same amounts. Same investments.

Month 12:

She logs in. She calculates her percentages.

Asset	Target	Actual
Equities	25%	27%
Bonds	25%	24%
Cash	25%	25%
Gold	25%	24%

She directs her next month's contributions to bonds and gold to bring them back to 25%.

She has completed her first year as an investor.

She has built the habit.

She is on her way.

What You've Built

After one year, Nonhlanhla has invested R6,000.

She has built a diversified portfolio worth slightly more (assuming some growth).

She has survived market ups and downs without panic.

She has learned to rebalance.

She is no longer someone who reads about investing.

She is an investor.

And in 10 years? She has R 102,422.

In 20 years? She has R 379,684

In 40 years? She has R 3.2m

That R500 a month will have grown into something substantial.

All because she started.

Your Portfolio at a Glance

Asset	ETF/Vehicle	What It Does
Equities	STX40	Grows during prosperity
Bonds	STXGOV	Protects during deflation
Cash	High-interest savings account	Saves you in emergencies and recessions
Gold	GLD	Protects during inflation and monetary crises

Key Takeaways

- The Permanent Portfolio divides your money equally among equities, bonds, cash, and gold
- Use low-cost ETFs available on local platforms like EasyEquities and SatrixNOW
- Rebalance once per year to sell high and buy low
- Use Tax-Free Savings Accounts for tax-efficient investing
- Stay disciplined through all economic cycles
- Your behaviour matters most

Try This Today

1. Open an EasyEquities account
2. Deposit R100 (or whatever you can afford)
3. Buy R25 of STX40 (equities)
4. Buy R25 of STXGOV (bonds)
5. Buy R25 of GLD (gold)
6. Move R25 to a high-interest savings account (cash)

You are now a Permanent Portfolio investor.

Congratulations.

Did You Know?

The JSE has been operating since 1887.

For more than 130 years, South Africans have been building wealth through the stock market.

You are joining a tradition that has survived wars, crises, and economic upheavals.

Reflection from the Stoics

Epictetus said: "First say to yourself what you would be; then do what you have to do."

You have now said to yourself: "I will be a disciplined investor. I will build a Permanent Portfolio. I will follow the plan."

The "doing" is where most people stop.

They love the idea but not the execution.

Execution is boring.

Execution is annual rebalancing, monthly contributions, and ignoring the noise.

But execution is also where the wealth is built.

Do what you have to do. The plan is nothing without the doing.

What You've Learned So Far

Chapter	Key Lesson
Introduction	You don't need to be rich to start. The habit matters more than the

	amount.
Chapter 1	Working hard is not enough. You need assets that work while you sleep.
Chapter 2	Inflation is the invisible thief. It steals from savers every day.
Chapter 3	Time is your superpower. Start early and let compounding work for you.
Chapter 4	Looking rich is not the same as being wealthy. Protect before you grow.
Chapter 5	The Permanent Portfolio prepares for all economic seasons. You don't need to predict the future.
Chapter 6	Equities are your running shoes. They provide growth during prosperity.
Chapter 7	Bonds are your winter coat. They protect you during deflations.
Chapter 8	Cash is your emergency backpack. It protects you when life goes wrong.
Chapter 9	Gold is your umbrella. It protects you during monetary storms.
Chapter	You now know exactly how to build

10	your Permanent Portfolio.

What's Next

In Chapter 11, we'll explore the most important part of investing: your behaviour.

You will learn:

- Why knowledge alone is not enough
- How greed and fear destroy portfolios
- The danger of FOMO and trend-chasing
- How to build good investing habits
- Why the most important investor is the one in the mirror

The next chapter is about mastering yourself—because your behaviour matters more than your intelligence.

CHAPTER 11: THE BRAIN IN YOUR WALLET

Behaviour Beats Intelligence

"No man is free who is not master of himself." — Epictetus

The Taxi Driver Who Became a Millionaire

Let me tell you about a taxi driver I met in Durban.

He drove a minibus from Umlazi to the city centre. Six days a week. Twelve hours a day.

He wasn't educated. He didn't have a degree. He didn't understand complicated financial jargon.

But he was a millionaire.

How?

Every day, he put R50 into a box. At the end of each

month, he deposited that money into an investment account.

He bought simple ETFs. He held them for years. He never sold.

He started when he was 25. By the time I met him at 55, he had built a comfortable retirement fund at over R 3m.

He wasn't clever. He was consistent.

He wasn't rich. He was disciplined.

He wasn't educated. He was committed.

Why Knowledge Alone Is Not Enough

You now know how to build a Permanent Portfolio.

You understand inflation, diversification, and the four economic seasons.

You have all the knowledge you need to become a successful investor.

But knowledge alone will not make you wealthy.

There are brilliant economists who lose money in markets.

There are PhDs who panic and sell at the bottom.

There are financial professionals who abandon their own plans when emotions take over.

Having a map doesn't help if you throw it out the window the moment the road gets bumpy.

Investing is not primarily an intellectual challenge.

It is a behavioural challenge.

The best portfolio in the world will fail if its owner cannot control their emotions.

The simplest, most boring strategy will succeed if its owner stays disciplined.

Greed and Overconfidence

When markets rise for several years, a dangerous feeling creeps in.

"I am a genius."

"This is easy."

"Why am I only investing R500 a month? I should borrow money to invest more."

"Everyone else is getting rich. I need to take more risk."

This is greed. This is overconfidence.

And it leads to disaster faster than a taxi driver skipping a red robot.

Greed tempts you to abandon your Permanent Portfolio for riskier bets.

It whispers that you are missing out.

It convinces you that the old rules no longer apply —that "this time is different."

But the rules always apply.

Markets do not rise forever. Every period of greed is followed by a crash.

The overconfident investors who borrowed to buy more lose everything.

The disciplined investors who stuck to their plan survive and eventually thrive.

Fear and Panic

If greed destroys portfolios during booms, fear destroys them during busts.

When markets crash, fear replaces overconfidence.

You check your portfolio daily. Each decline feels like a personal tragedy. News headlines scream disaster. Friends are selling. You want to sell too, just to stop the pain.

This is the moment that separates successful investors from everyone else.

Successful investors have a plan. They know crashes are normal. They know markets recover.

They hold their diversified portfolio and wait.

They might even buy more when prices are low.

Panicked investors sell at the worst possible moment. They lock in losses that would have recovered. They miss the rebound. They swear off investing forever.

Do not be a panicked investor.

The 2008 Story

Let me tell you about the 2008 financial crisis.

Markets fell 40%. People panicked.

I knew a fund manager who had built his entire reputation on picking the best-performing shares.

He was brilliant. He worked hard. He had a PhD in economics.

When the market crashed, he panicked.

He sold everything—shares, bonds, everything—and put it all in cash.

He missed the recovery.

He never rebuilt his reputation or his wealth.

Why did he panic?

Because he hadn't prepared for the possibility that he could be wrong.

He couldn't admit he didn't know what would happen next.

The Permanent Portfolio asks you to accept that you will be wrong sometimes. That you don't know everything. That the future is uncertain.

That humility is what saves you.

FOMO: The Fear of Missing Out

FOMO is the fear of missing out.

It is the feeling that others are getting rich while you are standing still.

You see friends posting about cryptocurrency

gains.

Your neighbours brag about their profits from the latest pyramid scheme (ibhanoyi) in your neighbourhood.

Colleagues talk about the hot new stock that doubled in a month.

Social media influencers brag about their trading profits—usually from a rented Lamborghini and a fake screenshots app.

FOMO whispers:

"You are a fool for holding a boring Permanent Portfolio. You should be making quick money."

Resist FOMO.

For every person who made money on a hot trend, ten more lost money.

For every lucky trade, there are hundreds of unlucky trades that never get posted on social media.

Permanent wealth is built slowly, not through gambling.

Your Permanent Portfolio will not make you rich overnight. It will make you wealthy over decades.

That is the trade-off you have chosen.

Accept it. Own it.

The Danger of Chasing Trends

Trend-chasing is the most common investing mistake.

Gold goes up for a few years. Suddenly everyone loves gold. You buy at the peak. Then gold crashes. You sell in disappointment.

Equities go up. Suddenly everyone is bullish. You increase your equity allocation. Then the market crashes. You sell at the bottom.

Every time you chase a trend, you buy after the price has already risen.

You are buying high.

Then you sell after the price falls. You are selling low.

This is the opposite of what successful investors do.

It's the financial equivalent of running into a burning building while everyone else is running out.

The Permanent Portfolio solves this by removing the need to chase.

You already own everything.

You already have exposure.

You do not need to chase anything.

The Media and Market Noise

Financial media exists to capture your attention, not to help you invest.

News channels need dramatic headlines.

"Market Crash!"

"Inflation Crisis!"

"Gold Rush!"

"New Technology Will Change Everything!"

Each headline creates urgency. Each headline tempts you to act. Each headline is designed to make you feel that you must do something—right now, before it's too late!

But the best thing you can do is usually nothing.

Turn off the financial news.

Unsubscribe from market prediction newsletters.

Block social media accounts that post about hot stocks.

The less noise you consume, the better your decisions will be.

Your portfolio doesn't need news. It needs peace.

Building Good Investing Habits

Discipline is not something you have or do not have.

Discipline is a set of habits.

Build these habits:

Habit	What to Do
Automate your investments	Set up a monthly debit order. You cannot

	forget. You cannot talk yourself out of it.
Check your portfolio less often	Once per month is plenty. Once per quarter is even better.
Rebalance on a fixed schedule	Choose one day per year. Do not rebalance any other time.
Avoid financial news	Unsubscribe. Unfollow. Mute.
Find an accountability partner	Discuss your plan with a sensible friend. Hold each other accountable.
Write down your investment policy	Put it on paper. Sign it. Read it when you are tempted to abandon your plan.

Your Investment Policy Statement

Here is a template.

Print it. Sign it. Stick it on your wall.

My Investment Policy

I, ______________________, commit to the following:

- I will hold 25% each in equities, bonds, cash, and gold

- I will rebalance once per year on [date]
- I will not sell during crashes
- I will ignore financial news and hot tips
- I will invest monthly, automatically
- I will check my portfolio no more than once per month

Signature: ________________________

Date: ________________________

The Investor in the Mirror

There is a famous saying in investing:

"The most important investor is the one in the mirror."

Your success will not be determined by the markets.

It will not be determined by the economy.

It will not be determined by interest rates or inflation or political events.

Your success will be determined by you.

By your ability to stick to a simple plan.

By your discipline when others panic.

By your patience when progress feels slow.

By your refusal to chase trends and hot tips.

By your commitment to showing up, month after

month, year after year.

The Permanent Portfolio is a tool.

You are the craftsman.

The tool only works if you use it correctly.

Be the investor who stays calm. Be the investor who stays disciplined.

Be the investor who builds wealth one month at a time.

Common Behavioural Mistakes

Mistake	Why It's Dangerous
Checking your portfolio every day	Creates anxiety and leads to bad decisions
Listening to financial news	Creates fear and encourages chasing trends
Following friends' tips	They don't know more than you do
Selling during crashes	Locks in losses you could have recovered
Borrowing to invest	Amplifies losses
Changing your plan every year	Prevents compounding from working

Key Takeaways

- Knowledge alone is not enough. Behaviour determines success

- Greed and overconfidence lead to risk-taking and losses
- Fear and panic cause selling at market bottoms
- FOMO tempts you to chase trends and buy high
- Ignore financial media and market noise
- Build habits: automate, check rarely, rebalance annually, avoid news
- The most important investor is the one in the mirror

Try This Today

1. Write down your investment policy
2. Sign it
3. Put it where you can see it
4. Tell someone about your plan
5. **Commit to being the investor in the mirror**

Did You Know?

The best investors in history are not the smartest.

They are the most disciplined.

Warren Buffett didn't get rich by being clever. He got rich by being patient.

Reflection from the Stoics

Epictetus taught that true freedom comes from mastering oneself.

The undisciplined investor is a slave:

- To greed
- To fear
- To the opinions of others
- To the news cycle

The disciplined investor is free.

When the market panics, the disciplined investor is unmoved.

When friends boast of quick gains, the disciplined investor feels no envy.

This is not coldness; it is strength.

It is the Stoic art of focusing only on what you can control:

- Your actions
- Your habits
- Your response

Master yourself, and you master your financial destiny.

What You've Learned So Far

Chapter	Key Lesson
Introduction	You don't need to be rich to start. The habit matters more than the amount.
Chapter 1	Working hard is not enough. You need assets that work while you sleep.
Chapter 2	Inflation is the invisible thief. It steals from savers every day.
Chapter 3	Time is your superpower. Start early and let compounding work for you.
Chapter 4	Looking rich is not the same as being wealthy. Protect before you grow.
Chapter 5	The Permanent Portfolio prepares for all economic seasons. You don't need to predict the future.
Chapter 6	Equities are your running shoes. They provide growth during prosperity.
Chapter 7	Bonds are your winter coat. They protect you during recessions.
Chapter 8	Cash is your emergency backpack. It protects you when life goes wrong.

Chapter 9	Gold is your umbrella. It protects you during monetary storms.
Chapter 10	You now know exactly how to build your Permanent Portfolio.
Chapter 11	Behaviour beats intelligence. Master yourself to master your financial destiny.

What's Next

In Chapter 12, we'll take the final step.

You will learn:

- How to take action starting today
- The story of Nomsa and Thabo—and the difference that action makes
- Your first R100 checklist
- What happens if you don't start—and what happens if you do

The next chapter is the shortest in the book. It's also the most important. Because everything you've read comes down to one thing: action.

CHAPTER 12: START NOW. START HERE.

Your First R100

"Don't explain your philosophy. Embody it." — Epictetus

The Moment of Truth

You have learned the principles.

You understand the strategy.

You know why inflation is the invisible thief.

You know how the Permanent Portfolio protects you.

You know that time is your superpower.

Now it is time to act.

This chapter is the shortest in the book.

It is also the most important.

Because everything you've read comes down to one thing:

Action.

Not tomorrow.

Not next month.

Not when you have more money.

Now.

The Story of Nomsa

Let me tell you about Nomsa.

Nomsa was 24 years old. She worked as a receptionist. She earned R8,000 a month.

She had read a book about investing. She understood the principles.

But she didn't start.

"I'll start next month," she said.

Next month came. And went. And came again.

She had reasons. Good reasons.

"I need to buy new shoes for work."

"My sister needs help with school fees."

"The car needs new tyres."

There was always a reason.

Five years later, Nomsa had still not invested.

She had spent more than R30,000 on things she couldn't remember.

She had nothing to show for it.

Nomsa didn't fail because she didn't understand investing.

Nomsa failed because she didn't start.

The Story of Thabo

Now let me tell you about Thabo.

Thabo was also 24 years old. He also worked as a receptionist. He also earned R8,000 a month.

He read the same book. He understood the same principles.

But Thabo started.

He opened an investment account. He set up a monthly debit order of R100.

Just R100. The equivalent of a few kota lunches.

He invested that R100 every month. Rain or shine. Good times or bad. Without fail.

Ten years later, Thabo had invested R12,000.

His portfolio had grown to more than R18,000.

It wasn't life-changing money. Yet.

But Thabo had built the habit.

He had learned to invest. He had learned to rebalance. He had learned to ignore the noise.

Thabo was on his way.

The Difference

Nomsa and Thabo were the same age. They earned the same salary. They had the same opportunities.

The only difference was action.

Nomsa waited for the perfect moment.

Thabo started with what he had.

Nomsa is still waiting.

Thabo is becoming wealthy.

Don't Wait, Start Now

Step 1: Open an Investment Account

You cannot invest without an investment account.

Fortunately, South Africa has excellent low-cost platforms designed for ordinary people.

EasyEquities

The most popular platform for new investors.

- You can buy fractional shares
- You can invest R100 even if one share costs R500
- User-friendly mobile app
- Low fees

How to open an account:

1. Go to easyequities.co.za
2. Click "Sign Up"
3. Enter your details (ID, proof of residence, phone number)
4. Complete FICA verification
5. Fund your account

It takes less than 15 minutes.

Action Item:

Open an EasyEquities account before the end of this week.

Not next month. Not next year.

This week.

Step 2: Build an Emergency Fund

Before you invest heavily, you need a small cash buffer.

This prevents you from needing to sell investments during emergencies.

Your first target: R5,000.

This will cover most small emergencies:

- A car repair
- A doctor's visit
- A broken phone
- An unexpected bill

Your second target: three months of essential ex-

penses.

This will take longer. Build it gradually.

But here's the important part:

While building your emergency fund, you can still invest small amounts.

Even R100 per month while you save for your emergency fund is better than nothing.

Action Item:

Open a high-interest savings account.

Set up an automatic transfer of whatever you can afford each month.

Step 3: Invest Every Month

Consistency matters more than amount.

Set up a monthly debit order.

From your bank account to your investment account.

Start with whatever you can afford:

- R100
- R200
- R500
- R1,000

Pay yourself first.

When your salary arrives, immediately move your investment amount to your investment account.

Treat it like any other bill.

Except this bill pays future you.

Action Item:

Set up a monthly debit order of at least R100 to your investment account.

Schedule it for the day after your salary arrives.

Step 4: Ignore the Headlines

Once you start investing, the noise begins.

Markets will rise. Markets will fall.

News headlines will scream disaster or euphoria.

Friends and family will share hot tips.

Social media will show people getting rich (or claiming to).

Ignore all of it.

Your plan is simple.

Your plan is boring.

Your plan works.

Do not let the noise distract you.

Action Item:

Unfollow financial influencers on social media.

Unsubscribe from market prediction emails.

If you must consume financial news, limit yourself to 15 minutes per week.

Enough to be informed.

Not enough to be influenced.

Step 5: Rebalance Once a Year

Once per year, on a specific date you choose, log into your investment account.

Check your allocations.

Calculate what percentage of your portfolio is in:

- Equities
- Bonds
- Cash
- Gold

If any asset is above 30% or below 20%, sell some of the overweight asset and buy more of the underweight asset to return to 25% each.

That's it.

One rebalancing per year.

Do not rebalance more often.

That way lies madness and transaction costs.

Action Item:

Put a recurring calendar entry for your rebalancing date.

Title it: "Permanent Portfolio Rebalancing."

Set it to repeat annually.

Real-Life Examples

Let me show you what this looks like for ordinary South Africans.

Sipho Invests R100 a Month

Sipho is a university student. He has very little money.

But he commits to R100 a month.

He opens an EasyEquities account.

He buys fractional shares of the four ETFs each month.

After one year, he has invested R1,200.

His portfolio has likely grown modestly.

But more importantly, the habit is formed.

After ten years, his R100 a month has grown significantly.

By the time he graduates and gets a full-time job, he can increase his contributions.

The habit is already automatic. Like brushing his teeth.

Nonhlanhla Invests R200 a Month

Nonhlanhla is a retail worker earning minimum wage.

She lives frugally.

She invests R200 a month.

She uses SatrixNOW for simplicity.

She buys R50 of each of the four ETFs every month.

After twenty years, her portfolio is substantial.

She has learned to live without that R200.

It is as automatic as her rent payment.

Wealth has grown quietly in the background while she worked, laughed, and lived her life.

Njabulo Invests R1,000 a Month

Njabulo is a young professional earning a decent salary.

He invests R1,000 a month.

He buys the four ETFs in equal proportions.

He also contributes to his company pension fund and a Tax-Free Savings Account.

After twenty-five years, Njabulo's portfolio has grown into significant wealth.

He could stop contributing and let it compound further.

He is on track for early financial independence.

The kind where working becomes optional, not necessary.

Nonkululeko Invests R2,000 a Month

Nonkululeko is a high earner.

She invests R2,000 a month into her Permanent

Portfolio.

She also maxes out her TFSA and contributes to a retirement annuity.

Her portfolio grows rapidly.

After fifteen years, she has options.

She could reduce her work hours.

Change careers.

Take a sabbatical.

Her investments provide freedom.

Not just money.

The power to choose.

What to Buy

For your first R100, here's exactly what to do.

Asset	Amount	ETF Code	What It Is
Equities	R25	STX40	40 largest JSE companies
Bonds	R25	STXGOV	South African government bonds
Cash	R25	Savings account	High-interest savings account
Gold	R25	GLD	Physical gold backed ETF

That's it.

You now own a Permanent Portfolio.

Start Before You Feel Ready

Here is the most important lesson in this book:

You will never feel ready.

There will always be a reason to delay.

"I need to pay off debt first."

"I need to build a bigger emergency fund."

"I need to learn more before I start."

"I will start next month."

These reasons are excuses.

They sound reasonable. They feel responsible.

But they are just fear dressed up as logic.

Like a wolf in a suit.

Start with what you have.

Start where you are.

Start today.

What Happens If You Don't Start

Let me show you what happens if you don't start.

You work hard.

You save what you can.

You keep your money in a bank account.

Inflation eats your savings year after year.

At age 65, you have less purchasing power than you started with.

You worked for 40 years.

You saved diligently.

And you have less than you started with.

That is the quiet tragedy of personal finance.

Not the people who try and fail.

The people who never try at all.

What Happens If You Do Start

Now let me show you what happens if you start.

You invest R100 a month.

You don't make big bets. You don't chase hot tips.

You simply invest consistently for 40 years.

At 10% growth, that R100 a month becomes:

- After 10 years: R20,500
- After 20 years: R75,900
- After 30 years: R226,000
- After 40 years: R632,400

That's R100 a month.

Not R1,000. R100.

The equivalent of a few kota lunches.

That's what consistency does.

The FOMO You Should Actually Fear

Everyone talks about FOMO: the fear of missing out on the hot investment.

But there's a FOMO that matters more:

The fear of missing out on your own future.

The fear of getting to 65 and realising you should have started.

The fear of watching your friends retire while you're still working.

The fear of knowing you had the opportunity and let it slip away.

That fear is real.

That fear is justified.

Don't let that be your story.

Your First R100 Checklist

Print this page. Put it on your mirror.

Check off each step as you complete it.

THIS WEEK:

☐ Open an EasyEquities account (15 minutes)

☐ Deposit R100

☐ Buy R25 each of STX40, STXGOV, GLD, and cash

THIS MONTH:

☐ Open a separate savings account for your emergency fund

☐ Transfer R100 (or whatever you can) to it

☐ Set up an automatic monthly transfer to EasyEquities for the day after payday

NEXT 6 MONTHS:

☐ Grow your emergency fund to R5,000

☐ Don't touch it unless you face a genuine emergency

☐ Keep investing your monthly R100 (or more) in the four ETFs

EVERY YEAR (from now on):

☐ On your chosen rebalancing date, check your percentages and rebalance

☐ Increase your monthly investment amount by whatever you can

☐ Even R20 extra helps

REPEAT UNTIL FINANCIALLY FREE:

☐ The habit beats the amount

☐ Start small, stay consistent, ignore the noise

Your First R100 Is the Most Important

Your first R100 is not about making money.

It's about making a statement. **To yourself:**

"I am the kind of person who starts."

"I am the kind of person who keeps promises to their future self."

"I am the kind of person who builds wealth."

Start small. Start now.

Your future self is already thanking you.

Key Takeaways

- Open an EasyEquities account this week
- Build a small emergency fund before investing heavily
- Set up a monthly debit order—pay yourself first
- Ignore financial news and hot tips
- Rebalance once per year on a fixed date
- Start with whatever you can afford, even R100 per month
- Do not wait until you feel ready. Start today

Try This Today

1. Open your phone
2. Go to easyequities.co.za
3. Sign up
4. Deposit R100
5. Buy the four assets
6. Set up a monthly debit order

You are now an investor.

Congratulations.

Did You Know?

- 80% of South Africans do not invest
- 80% of South Africans will struggle in retirement
- The 20% who invest will retire comfortably

You are now in the 20%.

You are on the right side of the numbers.

Reflection from the Stoics

Epictetus said:

"Don't explain your philosophy. Embody it."

This book has given you a philosophy of investing:

- Simple
- Diversified
- Disciplined
- Patient

Now you must embody it.

The smallest action is worth more than the grandest intention.

Open the account.

Set up the debit order.

Buy your first R100 of ETFs.

That act, small as it seems, is the moment you stop being someone who reads about investing and become someone who invests.

Embody the philosophy.

Let your actions speak.

What You've Learned So Far

Chapter	Key Lesson
Introduction	You don't need to be rich to start. The habit matters more than the amount.
Chapter 1	Working hard is not enough. You need assets that work while you sleep.
Chapter 2	Inflation is the invisible thief. It steals from savers every day.
Chapter 3	Time is your superpower. Start early and let compounding work for you.
Chapter 4	Looking rich is not the same as being wealthy. Protect before you grow.
Chapter 5	The Permanent Portfolio prepares for all economic seasons. You don't need to predict the future.
Chapter 6	Equities are your running shoes.

	They provide growth during prosperity.
Chapter 7	Bonds are your winter coat. They protect you during recessions.
Chapter 8	Cash is your emergency backpack. It protects you when life goes wrong.
Chapter 9	Gold is your umbrella. It protects you during monetary storms.
Chapter 10	You now know exactly how to build your Permanent Portfolio.
Chapter 11	Behaviour beats intelligence. Master yourself to master your financial destiny.
Chapter 12	Start now. Start here. Your first R100 is the most important step.

What's Next

You've reached the end of the practical chapters.

Now it's time to read the Conclusion—where everything comes together and you're invited to take the final step.

CONCLUSION: ONE DECISION CAN CHANGE YOUR FUTURE

"Waste no more time arguing what a good man should be. Be one." — Marcus Aurelius

The One Thing You Can Control

You cannot control the economy.

No one can. Not the President. Not the Governor of the Reserve Bank. Not the richest businessman in Sandton.

The economy is a complex, unpredictable system. Anyone who claims to know what will happen next is either deluded or dishonest—or selling you something.

You cannot predict the future.

Market crashes will come. Inflation will surge. Recessions will arrive. Booms will follow.

The sequence and timing are unknown.

Prediction is a fool's game, and you are no fool.

You cannot eliminate uncertainty.

Investing always involves risk. There is no guarantee. No strategy works perfectly in every single year.

Uncertainty is the price of admission for long-term growth.

But you can control something.

You can control your actions.

You can control your habits.

You can control your response to the world.

That is the most important step.

The Story of the Two Taxis

Let me tell you a story.

There are two taxis at the taxi rank.

Taxi A is driven by a driver who waits for the perfect moment.

He waits for traffic to clear. He waits for more passengers. He waits for the weather to improve.

He waits and waits.

The taxi never leaves.

Taxi B is driven by a driver who leaves immediately.

He knows the route. He knows there will be traffic. He knows the weather might change.

He leaves anyway.

The taxi gets where it's going.

The passengers on Taxi B arrive at their destination.

Taxi A never moves.

Investing is the same.

The people who wait for the perfect moment never leave the taxi rank.

The people who start with what they have get where they're going.

Start with what you have.

Leave the taxi rank.

What You Now Know

You now understand things that most South Africans never learn.

You understand that **working hard is not enough.** You need assets that work while you sleep.

You understand that **inflation is the invisible thief.** It steals from savers every single day.

You understand that **the Permanent Portfolio prepares for all economic seasons.** You don't need to predict the future to invest.

You understand the difference between **looking rich and being wealthy.**

You understand **equities** (your running shoes), **bonds** (your winter coat), **cash** (your emergency backpack), and **gold** (your umbrella).

You understand that **behaviour beats intelligence.** Your discipline matters more than your IQ.

You understand that **time is your superpower.** Every year you delay costs you hundreds of thousands of Rands.

You have the knowledge.

Now you need to act.

The Plan

Here is your plan.

Simple. Clear. Proven.

Save. Spend less than you earn. Every month. No exceptions.

Invest. Set up a monthly debit order. R100 is enough to start.

Diversify. Own 25% each in equities, bonds, cash, and gold.

Rebalance. Once per year. On the same date. Every year.

Ignore the noise. Turn off financial news. Unfollow social media "experts."

Be patient. Wealth is built one month at a time. It takes decades.

Start now. Not next week. Not next month. Today.

The Most Important Step

The most important step is the first one.

Not the perfect one.

Not the big one.

Not the one you take after you've saved enough, learned enough, or felt ready.

The first one.

That's all it takes.

Open the investment account. Deposit your first R100. Buy the four assets.

Set up the debit order.

That's it.

What You Can Achieve

Let me show you what's possible.

At 25 years old:

Invest R500 a month for 40 years at 10% growth.

- Total invested: R 240,000
- Final value: Approximately R 3.2million

At 30 years old:

Invest R500 a month for 35 years at 10% growth.

- Total invested: R 210,000
- Final value: Approximately R 1.9million

At 35 years old:

Invest R500 a month for 30 years at 10% growth.

- Total invested: R 180,000
- Final value: Approximately R 1.1million

What that could mean:

R 3.2million could:

- Pay off a house
- Fund a comfortable retirement
- Provide R20,000 a month in sustainable income
- Give you the freedom to choose your path

That's what starting early can achieve.

That's what consistency can achieve.

That's what discipline can achieve.

The Only Regret

I've met many investors over the years.

I've met wealthy investors. I've met struggling investors.

I've met investors who started early and investors who started late.

The ones with regrets are always the same:

They didn't start earlier.

No one ever says, "I started too early."

No one ever says, "I saved too much."

No one ever says, "I invested too consistently."

The only regret is not starting sooner.

Don't be that person.

The R100 Investor

You are now the R100 investor. That doesn't mean you only have R100.

It means you understand the most important lesson in investing:

You don't have to be rich to start.

You can start with whatever you have.

You can start small. You can start imperfectly. You can start with fear and uncertainty.

But you must start.

Your Invitation

This book is an invitation.

An invitation to join a different club.

Not the club of people who talk about wealth.

The club of people who build it.

Not the club of people who wait for the perfect moment.

The club of people who start.

Not the club of people who complain about the economy.

The club of people who build systems that work regardless.

The door is open.

Walk through it.

What You Do Now

Here is your final checklist.

Not for tomorrow. Not for next week.

For now.

TODAY:

☐ Open an investment account

☐ Deposit your first R100

☐ Buy R25 each of equities, bonds, cash, and gold

THIS WEEK:

☐ Set up a monthly debit order

☐ Open a high-interest savings account for your emergency fund

☐ Start building your R5,000 emergency fund

FOREVER:

☐ Invest every month without fail

☐ Rebalance once per year

☐ Ignore the noise

☐ Stay the course

Key Takeaways

- You cannot control the economy, but you can control your actions
- The most important step is the first one. Start today
- Small amounts invested consistently grow into large amounts over time
- The only regret investors have is not starting earlier
- You have the knowledge, the plan, and the tools
- The only thing missing is action
- **Start today**

Did You Know?

Most millionaires are not born wealthy.

Most millionaires are ordinary people who started investing early and stayed consistent.

They didn't inherit money.

They didn't win the lottery.

They didn't get lucky.

They built it. One month at a time.

You can too.

Final Reflection from the Stoics

Marcus Aurelius wrote:

"Waste no more time arguing what a good man should be. Be one."

You have argued enough.

You have read the book.

You have learned the principles.

You have understood the strategy.

Now be the investor.

Start today. Start small. Stay disciplined.

Build wealth one month at a time.

What You've Learned Throughout This Book

Chapter	Key Lesson
Introduction	You don't need to be rich to start. The habit matters more than the amount.
Chapter 1	Working hard is not enough. You need assets that work while you sleep.
Chapter 2	Inflation is the invisible thief. It steals from savers every day.

Chapter 3	Time is your superpower. Start early and let compounding work for you.
Chapter 4	Looking rich is not the same as being wealthy. Protect before you grow.
Chapter 5	The Permanent Portfolio prepares for all economic seasons. You don't need to predict the future.
Chapter 6	Equities are your running shoes. They provide growth during prosperity.
Chapter 7	Bonds are your winter coat. They protect you during recessions.
Chapter 8	Cash is your emergency backpack. It protects you when life goes wrong.
Chapter 9	Gold is your umbrella. It protects you during monetary storms.
Chapter 10	You now know exactly how to build your Permanent Portfolio.
Chapter 11	Behaviour beats intelligence. Master yourself to master your financial destiny.
Chapter 12	Start now. Start here. Your first R100 is the most important step.

Conclusion	One decision can change your future. Make that decision today.

Welcome to your journey.

ABOUT THE AUTHOR

Senzo J Hlangu

Senzo J. Hlangu is a seasoned investment professional with nearly 30 years of experience spanning South Africa, the broader African continent, and the United Kingdom. He is the Founder and Chief Executive Officer of Stable Growth Investments (SGI), a licensed asset management firm focused on developing gold-protected, inflation-resilient investment solutions for retail investors and financial advisors.

Over the course of his career, Senzo has held investment, research, and portfolio management roles at leading financial institutions, including Old Mutual Investment Group, Prudential Portfolio Managers, Liberty Life, Symmetry Multi-Managers, RMB Asset Management, and Southern Life. He also served as Founding Operations Director and

Portfolio Manager at Legacy Africa Fund Managers. His experience includes managing South African and African equity portfolios and conducting research across more than ten African stock exchanges. During a secondment in London with Prudential Portfolio Managers, he researched the role of commodities—particularly gold—in globally diversified multi-asset portfolios.

Senzo holds a Bachelor of Science in Economics and Statistics from the University of Cape Town and a Postgraduate Diploma in Financial Planning from the University of Stellenbosch Business School.

Passionate about Austrian economics, monetary history, and investor education, he is committed to making transparent, cost-effective, and stable investment solutions accessible to individuals, families, and their advisors.

www.ingramcontent.com/pod-product-compliance
Lightning Source LLC
LaVergne TN
LVHW010716061126
851857LV00014B/1217
* 9 7 8 1 0 4 8 3 3 2 0 1 8 *